D0274590

3   0007 257 6

What's in your Attic?

What's in your Attic?

Jonty Hearnden

What's in your Attic?

Created and designed by
Miller's Publications
The Cellars, High Street
Tenterden, Kent, TN30 6BN
Tel: +44 (0) 1580 766411
Fax: +44 (0) 1580 766100

First published in Great Britain in 2007
by Miller's, a division of Mitchell Beazley,
imprints of Octopus Publishing Group Ltd,
2–4 Heron Quays, London E14 4JP
Miller's is a registered trademark of
Octopus Publishing Group Ltd,
an Hachette Livre UK Company

ISBN 9781 84533 322 5

A CIP catalogue record for this book is
available from the British Library

Set in Bliss and Baskerville Classico

Colour origination by Spectrum Colour Ltd, England
Printed and bound in China by Toppan

Consultant Editor: Jonty Hearnden

Managing Editor: Valerie Lewis
General Editor: Melissa Garnier
Production Co-ordinator: Philip Hannath
Editorial Co-ordinator: Deborah Wanstall
Editors: Jo Thom, Theresa Bebbington
Picture Research: Harriet Couchman, Joanna Hill,
 Alexandra Lewis Wortley
Designer: Lisa Druggan-Cherry, Mark Winwood
Indexer: Sally Roots
Production: Peter Hunt
Jacket Design: Victoria Burley
Photographers: Paul Harding, Mark Winwood
Photography assistants: Melissa Hall, Mel Smith,
 Charlotte Smith

Cover photographs: Mark Winwood

Contents

How and Where to Sell

Having identified your objects and roughly established what they are worth, you then have to choose how to go about selling them. There are a number of possible options. The buying and selling of antiques is a market like any other, so the more information you have the better. The majority of dealers and auction houses you consult will be 'honest brokers', but there are opportunists out there, particularly on the internet and at car boot sales, who will get a bargain if they can. Drawing on the collective expertise of myself and a team of renowned specialists, the following pages have been designed to help you get as much as possible from the sale of your objects by giving clues and pointers to aid you to identify and value them. You will then be able to decide on the best place to sell your items.

There are both general and specialist auction houses. In a larger auction house, make sure you see someone from the relevant department. They will tell you about the item and give you a verbal or written opinion and price. The price will be on the low side to encourage buyers at the sale and is not intended as a target price. If the object is valuable you may agree a 'reserve'; this is a value below which the auction house will not sell. An auction house may be able to do a valuation from a good photograph.

There are specialist sales for particular subject areas, such as fashion, and you may want to wait for one of these rather than rush into the first general sale, where your item may not be seen to best advantage.

If you want to go ahead make sure that you read and understand the auction house's terms and conditions. All auction houses will charge a percentage commission on the hammer price (the price the object is sold for at the sale). There are other costs to consider: they will levy VAT on their commission, may also charge for insurance and for an illustration (if relevant). Some auction houses will charge a fee even if the item does not sell – always a possibility. If you have a selection of items, some too big to move easily, many auction houses will come and do a valuation.

Car boot sales can be hectic.

DEALERS

You may feel you would rather have the cash in hand and not wait for a sale, or risk the object not selling at auction, in which case go and talk to a dealer. Reputable dealers will offer a fair price as they are always looking for new stock to sell. Something that has not 'done the rounds' in the auction world but perhaps has a provenance (history) in your family may well be an attractive proposition. However, you need to have done your homework and know how much you want for your item.

Most reputable dealers will belong to one of two trade organisations, BADA and LAPADA, and this will be printed on their letterhead or advertisements featuring their business. LAPADA has a code of practice that all members must adhere to. A good recommendation often comes by word of mouth, maybe from friends who have used a dealer. Antiques Fairs are a good place to meet dealers and look at their stock. Take a good photograph with you to show. You can also post or email photographs to dealers who may then be willing to make an offer.

CAR BOOT SALES

For many of the less valuable items a car boot sale can be ideal. It is hard work so always go with a friend. Find out where the local boot sales are and go and have a look round. Some may be better than others. Check out items similar to the ones you are going to sell, and take note of the prices. You must have all your prices organized before you get to the boot sale. Opportunists will descend on you while you are still unloading things from the car in the hope of getting a bargain in the confusion.

THE INTERNET

You can get good prices, but you can also get ripped off. You must be computer literate, with a good enough digital camera to get really good images. Be honest with your descriptions or your rating (sales satisfaction indicator) will suffer. Repeatable objects, such as toy cars, are easier to sell over the net as their value is more apparent. Unique items are more difficult.

Having sold, you must be prepared to pack the item well so that it does not get damaged in the post. Find out how much the postage would be and pass this cost on to the buyer.

Jonty Hearnden

Selling at auction should give you an immediate return.

Potential buyers will view your lot before buying.

The Experts

Miller's would like to thank all the experts consulted for their time and knowledge in the preparation of this book. Our thanks are also due to Tim Malone of Gorringes Auctioneers, Lewes, Baldwin's Auctions, St James's Auctions, Robert Opie, Michael Bennett-Levy, and Raj Bisram of Bentley's Auctioneers, Cranbrook, for their assistance, particularly with photography.

Daniel Bexfield (Silver) has been dealing and specializing in antique silver for 25 years. He regularly contributes to television and radio programmes on silver and is the editor of *The Finial*, a magazine devoted to silver spoons.
Daniel Bexfield Antiques, 26 Burlington Arcade, London W1J 0PU Tel: 0207 491 1720
Email: antiques@bexfield.co.uk www.bexfield.co.uk

Roy Butler (Medals) is Senior Partner at Wallis & Wallis. He is the *Antiques Roadshow*'s Militaria expert and lectures regularly. He is also a member of the Military History Society and the Army Historical Research Society.
Wallis & Wallis, West Street Auction Galleries, Lewes, East Sussex BN7 2NJ Tel: 01273 480208 Fax 01273 476562
www.wallisandwallis.co.uk

Tim Davidson (Ephemera) has been an auctioneer for 23 years and the cigarette, trade card and ephemera expert for 16 years at T. Vennett-Smith Auctions. Trevor Vennett-Smith is one of the country's leading auctioneers of paper-based collectables.
T. Vennett-Smith Auctions, 11 Nottingham Road, Gotham, Nottingham NG11 0HE Tel: 01159 830541
Fax: 01159 830114 www.vennett-smith.com

Richard Garnier (Clocks) was for 17 years head of the Clock Department at Christie's, King Street, London before moving to Garrard's and later to Asprey's, Bond Street. He now a specialist in rare and interesting clocks and runs Clocksearch UK.
Tel: 01580 240426 Email: rich.garnier@tinyworld.co.uk

Glenn Butler (Diecast Toys) is a partner at Wallis & Wallis, Europe's oldest established Toy auction house, and is their expert on Toys and Models. He has worked for the BBC doing live radio programmes and the *Antiques Roadshow*.
Wallis & Wallis, West Street Auction Galleries, Lewes, East Sussex BN7 2NJ Tel: 01273 480208
www.wallisandwallis.co.uk

Paul Campbell (Ceramics and Metalware) formerly of Sotheby's, Billingshurst, is now Head of Ceramics and Glass and Associate Partner at Gorringes Fine Art Auctioneers. Member of the Royal Institute of Chartered Surveyors since 1999 and a regular contributor on antiques to *Woman's Weekly*.
Gorringes Lewes, 15 North Street, Lewes, E Sussex BN7 2PD Tel: 01273 472503 www.gorringes.co.uk

Brian Dunn (Jewellery) has worked in Hatton Garden, Garrard's and Asprey's. He is now an independent valuer, a tutor for the National Association of Goldsmiths and has chaired their Valuations Committee. He also advises the police.
Tel: 01580 892993
Email: dunn.enterprises@tesco.net

Leslie Gilham (Furniture) has had over 35 years experience in the world of auctioneering. He is Senior Auctioneer at Gorringes auction house, Bexhill, Sussex and consultant to Gorringes, Tunbridge Wells, Kent.
Terminus Road, Bexhill-on-Sea, East Sussex TN39 3LR Tel: 01424 212994 www.gorringes.co.uk

Katherine Higgins (Fashion) is an author, writer and broadcaster specializing in modern collectables. She started her career in the Press Office at Christie's and became the *Daily Express* correspondent on antiques. She has written for the *Sunday Times, Daily Mail* and *Daily Telegraph* and appears regularly on the BBC's *Antiques Roadshow.*
katherine@higgins-world.co.uk www.higginsworld.co.uk

David Lowrie (Cameras) owns, with his wife Beryl, the Otford Antiques and Collectors Centre. He specializes in cameras, vintage tools and antique guns.

Otford Antiques & Collectors Centre, 26-28 High Street, Otford, Kent TN14 5PQ
Tel: 01959 522025 www.otfordantiques.co.uk

Lisa Norfolk (Coins) has been General Editor of *Miller's Antiques Price Guides* since 1995. After graduating in French from Cardiff University, she trained as a numismatist (coin specialist) at Stanley Gibbons, subsequently moving to B. A. Seaby Ltd and finally Christie's, King Street.
Lisnumis@aol.com

Manfred Schotten (Sporting) is originally from Bavaria and moved to England in the 1970s. He has been specializing in Sporting Antiques for over 25 years at his premises in Burford, Oxfordshire.
Manfred Schotten Antiques, 109 High Street, Burford, Oxfordshire OX18 4RG Tel: 01993 822302
Email: admin@schotten.com

Pepe Tozzo (Modern Technology) has been interested in technology from the 1970s when Clive Sinclair's early calculators fired his imagination. He wrote *Collectable Technology,* published in 2005, and regularly appears on both TV and radio.
Email: info@hampshirepictures.co.uk www.tozzo.co.uk

Colin Lewis (Dolls & Games) became interested in toys and dolls with a collection of Victorian automatons, which progressed to bisque dolls, German tinplate, diecast toys and Japanese toys. He then set up The Magic Toy Box, which he still runs.

The Magic Toy Box, 210 Havant Road, Drayton, Portsmouth, Hants PO6 2EH Tel: 02392 221307
Email: magictoybox@btinternet.com

Andy McConnell (Glass) appears on the BBC's *Antiques Roadshow* and has written for *The Times, Country Life* and BBC's *Homes & Antiques.* He has written *The Decanter, An Illustrated History of Glass from 1650,* and *20th Century Glass.*

Glass Etc 18-22, Rope Walk, Rye, East Sussex TN31 7NA
Tel: 01797 226600 www.decanterman.com

Ian Pout (Teddy Bears) became an antiques dealer in 1974 and opened the UK's first shop specializing in new and old bears. His collection includes the record-breaking Alfonzo, bought for £12,100. The annual catalogues featuring over 400 bears have become collectors items in their own right.

Teddy Bears, 99 High Street, Witney, Oxon OX28 6HY
Tel: 01993 706616 Email: jan@witneybears.co.uk

Hugh St Clair (Pictures) trained at Sotheby's and worked in a number of auction houses. He is a well respected journalist in the field of fine and applied arts and has written three *Miller's Picture Price Guides* and *Miller's Guide to Affordable Art.* He advises on all aspects of art including restoration, purchase and sale.

98 Saltram Crescent, London W9 3JX Tel 0208 960 9537

Susanna Winters (Books) qualified in History of Art and Architecture, English Literature and the Visual Arts. She has worked for the National Trust, Blackwell's Rare Books in Oxford and is now at Dominic Winter Book Auctions.

Dominic Winter Book Auctions, Mallard House, South Cerney, Glos GL7 5UQ Tel: 01285 860006 www.dominicwinter.co.uk

Furniture

Chairs, Tables, Chests of Drawers, Bookcases and Display Cabinets

Despite the recent changes in fashion and a much publicized rejection of old furniture in favour of a more modern look, a high proportion of homes still contain antique pieces, many of which have long family histories.

ALTHOUGH it is unlikely that you will stumble across a major 18th-century or even 19th-century item of furniture such as a Chippendale chair shrouded in dust in your attic, it is quite possible that granny's old chair or side table is worth a second glance. It should certainly be rescued from the ignominy of the local charity shop, car boot sale or the back garden bonfire.

With all furniture, condition and quality are the two main factors that will dictate the value of any piece. You should be aware that a lot of the more utilitarian antique pieces have been modified over the years for reasons of simple practicality – it might have been too big, too small or no longer fulfilled the function required, so it was altered. Added to this, some objects might have been damaged and badly repaired, while others might have been allowed to gently fall apart. These alterations and repairs will affect the value.

As a rule of thumb, the general quality of furniture declined following the advent of mass production that occurred around 1830. However, many impressive items continued to be made in traditional styles up to the outbreak of WWI.

So, what are you most likely to stumble over in the attic or in the family home that is about to be vacated after many years? Well, due to the sheer quantity produced, Victorian furnishings are the most common items: chests of drawers, work tables, parlour chairs, balloon-backed dining chairs and hall stands. Although many of these will have only limited financial value in the current market, they may well be worth keeping in the family, as it is likely that the market will in due course change again and these items could come back into fashion. In any event, you should never commit anything to the skip unless you are absolutely certain what it is or you have checked with an expert.

Different types of wood commonly used for furniture making – the type of wood may help you to identify and date your piece of furniture.

SHOP WINDOW
Good quality pieces in today's market

One of a set of six ash and elm Windsor chairs, by I. Godfrey, c1830.
£5,000–5,500

One of a set of eight Chippendale-style mahogany dining chairs, c1920.
£5,000–5,500

Mahogany bergère chair, c1825.
£2,500–2,800

Rosewood breakfast table, early 19thC.
£650–800

£1,100–1,300

Regency mahogany, satinwood and ebony-strung secretaire bookcase.
£4,000–4,500

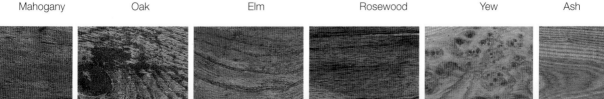

| Mahogany | Oak | Elm | Rosewood | Yew | Ash |

Woodseat and Dining Chairs

If you are fortunate enough to possess a 17th- or early 18th-century stool or chair, you may not be aware of just how much potential value you may be sitting on, regardless of the condition in which you have found it. However, most homes are more likely to possess seated furniture from the 19th or 20th centuries.

THERE IS still demand for simple pieces such as good woodseat chairs. Of these, the classic Windsor chair is the best known. There are wide regional variations in design, but most have solid elm seats and ash frames. The best use rarer timber for the frames, as with fruitwood in Mendlesham chairs from Suffolk and, perhaps most prized of all, yew in the high-backed chairs of Yorkshire. Signs of age and loving wear, such as the raised grain in a seat that has been worn and polished by much sitting on (*see below*), is prized.

Detail of plugged elm seat.

You should look for the patina that goes with age and the soft lines of hand-crafted backs or struts; later machine-made examples will have sharper angles. Any breaks or repairs will have a heavy effect on the value of chairs. Some chairs will have had arms added to increase their value (look for signs of different wood).

Interest in more formal dining chairs begins with sets of eight with values increasing as the number in each set grows. Late Georgian and early Victorian rosewood or mahogany examples are popular because they tend to be well made and better able to cope with a fidgety diner than the delicately proportioned balloon-backed walnut example on slender cabriole legs. Single chairs, or pairs, generally have very little value at the moment. Painted chairs such as *faux* bamboo, French country or Swedish, are decorative and, if robust, will have a value. Children's chairs may have some novelty value but unless 19th-century or earlier will not be worth a great deal.

Any repairs, particularly splicing or replacement of legs will greatly diminish the value of pieces. Woodworm will substantially affect the value, too. You should not undertake any restoration yourself. A bad repair may be impossible to undo. Restoration by an expert is expensive, and you will almost certainly not get your money back if you sell. It may be worth more to a dealer broken.

WHAT TO LOOK FOR...

What wood is used? Rosewood and mahogany would suggest Georgian or early Victorian. Walnut was reintroduced from the 1840s.

Are the corners of the seat braced with a thin piece of wood glued diagonally across the corner or a solid block screwed into the corner? The glued piece dates from the 18th century, while a screwed-on wood block dates from the 19th century onwards.

Is your mahogany chair heavy? Chairs from the 18th century are generally heavier than 19th-century examples.

Is it carved? The carving in the 18th century was much deeper than that of the 19th century.

If walnut or fruitwood, has it been affected by woodworm? Woodworm can seriously devalue it.

Elm and fruitwood Windsor chair,
with pierced splat and turned legs,
part of a set of six, early 19thC.
£400–600

Has no **arms**. Worth less than
a chair with original arms.

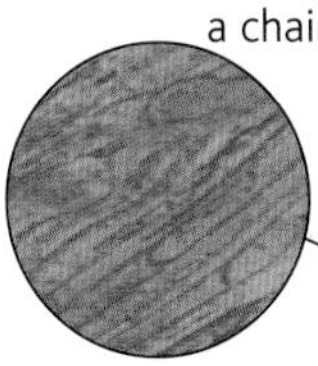

The **back**
has a soft rounded
appearance showing it was
hand made. The precise
right-angles of modern
machine-made examples
are worth less.

The grain on the elm
seat is raised – a good
sign, since the soft
'springwood' of the
annular ring shrinks
with age, leaving the
harder 'autumnwood'
standing proud.

Stretchers are unbroken –
a broken one will reduce
value but not worth
restoring if you are going
to sell.

Joints should be
glued, not nailed
or screwed.

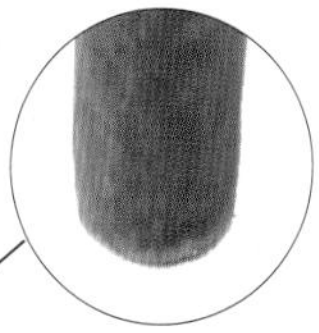

The **feet** show minor signs of
wear – does not reduce value.
Value will be reduced if they
have been cut down or capped.

WHAT HAVE YOU GOT?

Child's
bentwood chair,
c1910.
£120–150

One of a pair
of *faux* bamboo
chairs with
rush seats,
19thC.
£180–200

Mahogany
hall chair,
c1830.
£300–350

One of a set
of six pine
kitchen chairs,
19thC.
£300–400

One of a set of six
mahogany bar-
back dining chairs,
c1870.
£1,500–1,750

One of a set of
eight Victorian
mahogany
balloon-back
dining chairs.
£2,000–2,400

Upholstered Chairs, Sofas and Stools

The majority of upholstered chairs, sofas and stools have fallen in value as people prefer modern alternatives. However, stylish chairs of good quality, with a nice wood frame, do still command good prices.

COMFORT, quality and style are important elements in upholstered furniture, with decorative woods such as walnut, rosewood and mahogany being the most popular. Buyers look for cabriole legs rather than simple turned legs, but nothing too lumpy, and stylish details such as good, deep carving. Crisp bold acanthus carving may well add to value.

Most sofas are more or less unsaleable, with the exception of Chesterfields with their original leather covering, which are sought after, and some stylish chaise longues. Wing chairs with their comfortable, clubbable associations are also very popular. The upholstery itself is not important, and may well need redoing (*see right*). This can be expensive, and if you are selling a chair it may well be worth leaving the buyer to reupholster to suit his own taste. It will not significantly affect the price. If you do reupholster, try to keep to the same period as the chair when choosing the material.

The quality and robustness of the frame is a primary consideration. Obviously, a chair of any age will have been reupholstered a number of times. The frame may well be peppered with the holes of upholstery nails. This is a good indicator of age and, since it is covered by the upholstery, should not be restored. All the joints should be pegged and glued, and they may need reglueing. Get it professionally done by a restorer. If any of the joints have split or been broken, the value will be greatly reduced.

In the 19th century many copies were made of French gilded chairs and, though not fashionable now, they were well made. Their condition is important in valuing them, and if the gilding has been worn down with use do not try to replace it with gold paint.

The most common form of upholstered chair – the show wood chair – with a frame surrounding an upholstered back and seat, are not much sought after unless they are particularly stylish. Modern copies made in the Far East are often too crisply carved and the wood looks dull. They are worth very little.

Small stools have little or no value. However, big Victorian stools, maybe 48in (120cm) long with cabriole legs, are fashionable fireside adornments, as are some early Victorian X-frame stools.

Characteristic holes and channels caused by woodworm. If there is dust on the floor beneath the item the woodworm may be live and the piece should be treated.

WHAT TO LOOK FOR...

How robust is the frame? If it 'rocks', it may need reglueing.

Has the frame been repaired? If so, the value has been reduced.

If carved, is the carving crisp and stylish? Quality carving adds to value.

What wood was used? Better woods add to value.

If painted or gilded, has the decoration been damaged? Some wear is an acceptable sign of age. Do not repaint it.

Are they cabriole or simple turned legs? The more stylish the more desirable.

Mahogany wing chair,
by Howard & Sons,
c1900. The name of the
maker, well-known for
their quality armchairs,
increases value. It is in
an earlier style and would
be easy to confuse with
an earlier 18thC piece
that would be much
more valuable.
£1,200–1,400

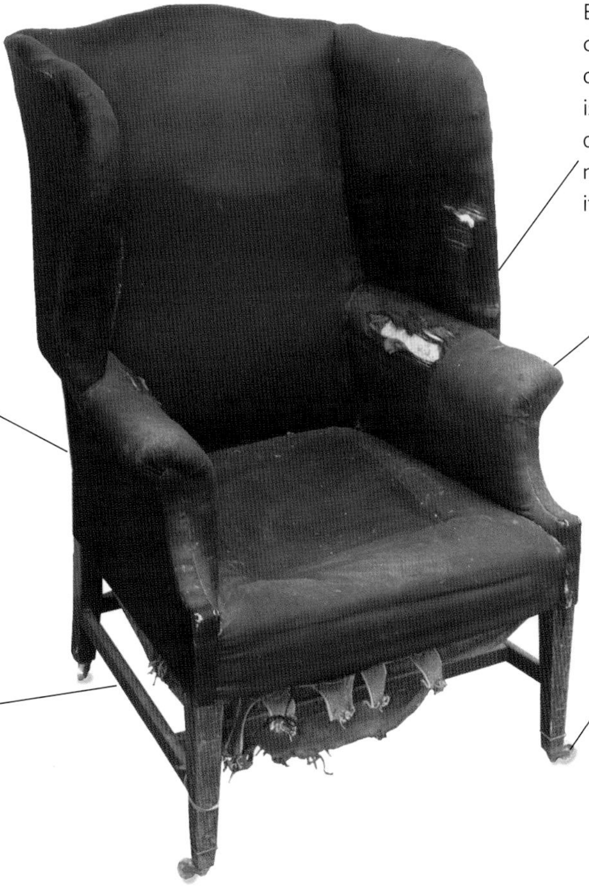

Even with worn fabric and
distressed upholstery, this
chair still holds value. This
is due to quality and style
of frame, along with the
maker's name which gives
it even more added value.

A robust frame is
essential. Gently test
arms and wings. Look
for woodworm
damage as this can, if
unchecked, weaken
the frame.

Look at the **frame** under
the upholstery if possible
to ensure the wood has
not split or been broken,
as this will greatly reduce
the value.

Older **casters** tend
to be quite small.
Check that legs
have not been
damaged by the
casters being
replaced with larger,
modern ones.

Stretchers should be
robust and undamaged.

WHAT HAVE YOU GOT?

French-style
gilded bergère
chair,
late 19thC.
£100–150

Rosewood stool
with woolwork
upholstery,
19thC.
£180–220

Victorian walnut
chaise longue, with
buttoned back and
bolster cushion.
£380–460

Victorian
rosewood
armchair on
casters.
£600–700

Victorian mahogany
nursing chair, by
Ross & Co, Ireland.
£650–750

Tables

As with much other wood furniture, tables have generally come down in value. There are a few notable exceptions, which are related to fashionable 'lifestyle choices'. Large dining tables and refectory tables that require the large sets of chairs (*see p12*), are in demand, whereas small occasional tables with their associations with front-room clutter are not.

MOST HOMES have a range of tables, from dressing table to kitchen table, but only a few are worth selling. Quality, workmanship and type of wood are deciding factors when it comes to value. Buyers will look for the patina of age, surfaces lovingly polished but slightly worn with use over time.

Tables are designed for practical use and many are damaged in the process. Table tops are vulnerable to marking, denting and scratching. Some slight damage may be a good sign of authenticity but

Victorian trumpet-shaped work table.

anything more serious, such as a crack or a burn, will diminish the value. Try to determine if the top has been replaced, perhaps in a different wood or style from the feet – look at the underside. With drop leaf and gateleg tables always look for any unexplained screw holes or changes in wood colour. Similarly, look for the swing mark of the supporting leg on the underside of the flap. There should be only one 'track' – if there are more, it was altered, which reduces value. Feet or legs may have been damaged – for example, tripod feet may collapse if too much weight is put on them, and this also affects value.

Many work and side tables have small drawers. Work table drawers should have well-fitted compartments. If well made, they will run smoothly without sticking and they should be glued, not screwed. If any screws have been used in the construction, look to see whether the cross-cut on the head is absolutely central – 18th-century screws were not mass-produced so the cross-cut was off centre.

Late Victorian furniture was often poorly finished as quality was often sacrificed.

WHAT TO LOOK FOR...

What wood has been used? Finer woods indicate better quality and higher value.

How heavy is it? A solid wood table will be heavy.

Is it solid or veneered? Veneered usually indicates better quality.

Has it been altered? Look underneath the top for any changes in wood colour (signs that struts were moved) or unexplained screw holes. These indicate an alteration and reduce value.

Has the underside of the top been stained, painted or polished? If so then something may well have been covered up.

Has the top been damaged or split? This reduces value.

Is it less than 29–30 inches (74–65cm) tall? It may have been cut down to make an occasional table.

If it has thin fragile legs or a tripod base, have any of the legs been broken? This reduces value.

If it is a large table that extends, does it have the extra leaf/leaves? Missing leaves reduce value.

Mahogany drop-leaf table,
with detachable leaf, early 19thC.
Use of mahogany, with attractive
grain, is an asset.
£1,200–1,500

Damage to the wood of the **flap**
where it closes will reduce the
value but can be restored.

Fine, **well-turned
legs** denote good
quality, but both
gateleg and drop
leaf tables suffer
from 'too many
legs'. which get in
the way of diners.

Look at the
underframe for
damage. A repair
may be covered up
with stain.

Freize at either
end with
moulding is
a sign of
good quality.

Casters – are
they original?
Do they match?

WHAT HAVE YOU GOT?

Oak gateleg table with
baluster legs, late
19th/early 20thC.
£100–200

Tilt-topped
mahogany
tripod
table,
c1780.
£350–450

Large pine kitchen
table, with two
drawers, on squared
legs, in good
condition, c1910.
£400–500

Victorian mahogany
side table,
with two drawers,
on reeded legs with
casters.
£550–600

Victorian mahogany
extending table, with
telescopic action
and three
extra leaves.
£1,800–2,200

Chests of Drawers

Made in huge quantities after the mid-19th century, chests of drawers are much less common before that date. Quality is all. The best examples have a thin top with a nicely moulded edge, four long drawers, perhaps with a brushing slide that pulls out immediately under the top, drawers that graduate (getting deeper as they go down) and an oak carcass.

OTHER SIGNS of quality are legs that splay out slightly at the bottom and drawers that slide easily. Size often equates with date: smaller equals earlier, larger later. Some also have boxwood inlay, but this is rare. Bowfront chests of drawers are often good quality and sell quite well.

Cheaper chests of drawers have a thicker top with a sharp machine-cut edge, three long and two short drawers, and straight legs or bun feet. If your chest of drawers has three short drawers at the top, there is a possibility it is half of a chest-on-chest, and has had a top and feet added. The drawer fronts are often solid mahogany and the top will not match. Not worth very much.

Original handles enhance value. Ring handles with an embossed backplate, gilded and lacquered, are the most common. Polishing them over the years will leave a mark on the wood. Later Victorian chests of drawers have turned wood bun handles and feet.

Small pine chests of drawers, painted or grained to look like oak, were originally used in servants' rooms. If found now, in their original state, there is a strong possibility their value is greater than the stripped and waxed version.

Damage to the legs, water damage to the top and veneer splitting off are common problems that reduce value.

Detail of a straight (right-angled, machine-made) edge.

Detail of a more rounded, moulded edge that is hand-crafted.

WHAT TO LOOK FOR...

What wood has been used? Veneer is usually a sign of better quality.

How many drawers? Four long drawers are best. The drawers should graduate in size, with the largest at the bottom.

Does the top have a moulded edge? This is a sign of good quality.

Are the handles or knobs original? Look for any shadow on the drawer front left by a different shaped handle, and look inside for any redundant screw holes that might have belonged to a different handle.

Does it have a pine or oak carcass? Oak is best and therefore worth more. Pine often reacts to central heating by splitting and warping.

Do the drawers slide in and out easily? You should be able to open them smoothly, with one handle, without sticking. The drawers should be dovetailed, not made with butt joints and screws.

Is the inside of the drawer stained or painted? This may indicate that something has been covered up or altered.

Victorian chest of drawers.
This mahogany chest of drawers has two short and three long drawers with bun handles. Four long drawers would indicate better quality, as would ring handles. **£400–600**

Look at the **carcass** to ensure joints are sound. It should not rock.

The **top** has a straight edge: a moulded top would be of better quality and therefore more valuable.

Bun **handles** indicate it is Victorian. Look inside the drawers to see if they are original.

Wood used is mahogany – is it solid or **veneered**? Veneered is better.

Look inside the **drawers**: are they dovetailed and glued? Screws or nails indicate a later date or a later repair and this will diminish value.

It has bun **feet**. A better quality chest of drawers might have outward sweeping feet.

WHAT HAVE YOU GOT?

G-Plan chest of drawers, Denmark, c1960.
£80–100

A mahogany bowfronted chest of drawers, c1800.
£500–700

Small, stripped pine chest of drawers, c1890.
£120–150

Walnut chest of drawers, late 19th century.
£400–450

Bookcases and Display Cabinets

Bookcases would have been in many homes from the mid-18th century, but purpose-built display furniture only became common in the mid- to late-19th century, with the new Victorian passion for collecting. Originally the province of serious collectors of coins or small works of art, the display cabinet became the focus of middle-class drawing rooms.

CREDENZAS, or side cabinets, frequently in walnut, inlaid with marquetry, and with ormolu mounts, were created specially for display. By the late 19th century sheets of glass were cheaper and available in larger pieces, so the front of better-quality credenzas consist of a single piece of glass. Their poorer quality cousins, the Edwardian display cabinets, have smaller panes and thin, square, tapered legs.

If you have a glazed cupboard, beware – it may be the top half of a bureau bookcase. Check underneath: it will either sit flat on the floor or will have had feet added. Look for different woods. With bureau bookcases which have a detachable top and bottom look out for 'marriages', where a bureau and a bookcase that do not belong together have been matched up – they will be worth much less. Again, look for different woods. Older pine or oak corner cupboards converted into display cabinets in the 19th century by glazing the doors are also common. Today, these have little value.

With the revival of the farmhouse kitchen 'look', pine or oak dressers – with or without glazed side doors – are today in demand. Designed to store and display china in a country setting, they are rustic versions serving the same purpose as a big mahogany bookcase. Unglazed stepped front bookcases are also popular.

Many display cabinets are fragile with thin legs and fine glazing bars. Glazing patterns may give you a clue as to the date. The glazing bars are easily damaged but it is rarely worth restoring before selling; leave it to the buyer. The same goes for cracked or broken panes: if it is old glass, it needs replacing with old glass.

Small display cabinets and glazed corner cupboards are no longer in demand. However, big breakfront bookcases still continue to sell well.

Fine, moulded glazing bars are a sign of quality.

WHAT TO LOOK FOR...

What wood has been used? The Victorians loved mahogany. Light woods such as satinwood were used in the Edwardian and later periods.

Is it solid wood or veneered? The best examples are usually veneered.

If it stands on thin legs, have they been broken? Broken legs, or ones that have started to twist, will reduce the value.

If glazed, look at the glazing bars. If they are thin and moulded, they are of good quality.

Are there many small panes? This is a useful indicator of date. Small panes were used in the 18th century and again by the Edwardians, larger panes by the Victorians.

If in two parts, do they belong together? Compare the wood and quality of workmanship. If they do not match up, the piece may be a 'marriage' of two different components, which will diminish the value.

Is the interior lined with the original velvet? If so, this is a definite plus. Do not replace it with new velvet!

Edwardian mahogany display cabinet, with inlay, on elegant splayed legs.
£300–500

Glazing pattern indicative of an Edwardian date – less valuable.

Use of mahogany **veneer** is a sign of good quality.

A good, well-moulded **cornice** adds to value.

Is the **inlay** decorative and extensive? Or, (less good), is it painted on to imitate, for example, boxwood stringing?

Thin **legs** are vulnerable to damage. These are unbroken and do not twist, and will help saleability.

Cracked **panes** diminish value slightly.

WHAT HAVE YOU GOT?

Oak corner cupboard with later glazing, c1850.
£150–180

Victorian pine bookcase with two lower doors.
£250–300

A mahogany breakfront low bookcase. c1890.
£500–600

Corner cabinet, c1910.
£600–700

Walnut vitrine, the door flanked by columns. c1850.
£700–800

Mahogany bureau bookcase, c1790.
£800–1,200

Pictures

Oil Paintings, Watercolours and Prints

Whether you like or loathe a particular picture is an entirely personal reaction, so judging whether your picture is of any value can be difficult. We are all haunted by the idea of selling something for £45 at a car boot sale, only to see it coming up for sale at a major auction house with a huge price tag. The best way to avoid this is to do your homework thoroughly.

MUCH OF the value of any picture will be determined by the artist. Look for a signature or perhaps a gallery label on the back of your picture. If you can see a name, do some research to find out as much as you can about the artist. Look in reference books, libraries or search through websites such as www.artnet.com (though you will have to subscribe). Your artist may have been involved with a movement or school, such as the St Ives School or the Bloomsbury Group, which will make your picture more interesting to collectors. Find out if the artist's work can be found in museums. Many museums have their own websites that you can browse. A dealer will almost certainly pay good money if you can show that other works by the same artist are in a museum.

If you do not know the artist, take your picture to an auction house and ask their expert for an opinion. Follow up their suggested attribution – you will need to do the research, as they do not have time. If you still cannot identify the artist, open competition between bidders at an auction is the best chance of getting a good price.

Having found out as much as you can about your picture, the next thing you will need to do is decide where to sell it. A pretty landscape may do well in a general sale at your local auction house but if, for example, you are selling a set of hunting prints, a specialist sale of sporting art may be better if you want to achieve a higher price. Look on the internet for listings of sales by all the auction houses. A gallery or dealer might buy from you, but you need to be sure of what you are selling. The same goes for selling at a car boot sale.

The art market is international and works of art sold at auction may be viewed and bought by a collector on the other side of the world. Even though the old masters may still command impressive prices, they are being overtaken by late 19th- and early 20th-century artists whose styles tend to be more impressionistic or abstract. This is reflected in the art market generally, where 'good' pictures by Victorian artists are much less sought after than they were, while little-known abstract artists are avidly collected. Irish and Russian painters, perhaps because of the current strength of these countries' economies, are now much sought after and collected.

Oil Paintings

Oil paintings are generally painted on canvas, but occasionally on board. Both are acceptable as long as they are in good condition. Oil paint is normally applied with a brush, but occasionally with a palette knife and, depending on the technique, you may be able to see individual brushstrokes. Many are also varnished, which may yellow over time, darkening the picture. Do not be tricked by an oleograph print, which has a canvas texture printed into it and is worth very little.

WHAT TO LOOK FOR...

Is it signed? The significance of a well-known artist will add considerably to the value of the painting.

What is its provenance? If you know anything about its history it will add interest.

What style is it in? Some styles are more fashionable.

If bought recently do you have the gallery receipt? This helps to identify the painter and improves value.

Is the artist an RA (Royal Academician)? If the artist belongs to a society has exhibited widely in his lifetime and/or if his work is in a major national collection, the painting will be worth more.

VALUE will not necessarily be a reflection of how old an oil painting is, but buyers will be attracted to a painting if you know its history (provenance), such as when and how it came into your family. Identify, if you can, the artist and find out as much as you can about them.

Buyers will often go for an attractive subject, such as a landscape or still life with flowers, rather than, for example, a gloomy Victorian parlour or kitchen scene, no matter how well painted. Certain subjects such as dogs and horses have a niche market. Pictures that have decorative qualities are also desirable, and are proving popular with interior designers. Record auction prices are being achieved by paintings in naïve, impressionistic and abstract styles.

Oil paintings are nearly always framed and the frame itself may have a value. If the frame is contemporary with the painting it may enhance its value. The auction houses occasionally have frame sales and it may be worth consulting past sale catalogues to see if your frame has a value.

Famous artists have always had their work faked and sometimes even the experts have been fooled. In some cases the fakes are so good –

for example those by Tom Keating after Samuel Palmer – that they are now worth a good deal in their own right.

While oil paintings do not fade in the sun, paint can flake off, bituminous areas crack and the canvas can rip if pressed or knocked. Oil paintings can be restored by an expert, but this is generally expensive and best left to the buyer to decide. If the varnish has discoloured, the surface dirt can be removed by a professional cleaner but collectors may prize the original condition.

Detail of Victorian 'perfect' brushwork.

Detail of impressionistic brushwork.

Cracking in the glaze.

Walter Wallor Caffyn, **Haytime at Winchfield (Hants),**
oil on canvas, dated 1889, 12 x 20in (30.5 x 52cm).
The title is inscribed by the artist on the reverse.
£2,000–2,500

The **place** is able to be identified. With a landscape subject this will help the value.

Subject is light and open, not dark and depressing. It has a depth and openness which is immediately attractive. Enhances value.

Some whitish **bloom** on varnish may slightly reduce value.

Caffyn is not a well-known artist so does not enhance the value.

The picture is signed. An authentic **signature** will add considerably to the value of the picture.

WHAT HAVE YOU GOT?

Charles H. Chapman, *The Falls of the Mawdach*, titled and dated 1894, oil on canvas.
£180–220

Imogen Collier, *Cheap Jack*, oil on canvas, signed, early 20thC.
£350–400

Sir Oswald Birley *Portrait of Rt Hon William*, signed and dated 1927, oil on canvas.
£500–600

Stanley Cursiter, *A Still Life of Red and Yellow Roses*, signed and dated 1958, oil on board.
£1,000–1,200

Frederick Gore *Hibiscus on a Covered Terrace*, signed, oil on canvas.
£2,800–3,300

Jack Morocco, *Barracuda, Port Lucaya*, signed, late 20thC, oil on canvas.
£3,000–3,600

Watercolours

Watercolours are generally on paper, with thin washes of colour applied with a brush. Some artists also used chalk to highlight areas, or pen and ink or, in the 20th century, gouache. The great thing about watercolour is the way in which it depicts light. Northern European light and cloudy skies lend themselves perfectly. The best watercolours have a translucency and textural quality that cannot be achieved in any other medium.

Watercolour by Edward Seago (1910–74), entitled *High Pasture*, **£4,500–5,000**.
Look at how he paints the sky, achieving a wonderful luminosity.

WATERCOLOURS are usually smaller and more portable than oil paintings and were often less expensive to buy and therefore are found in a greater variety of homes.

The artist's name is the biggest clue to value. Look for a signature or label that identifies the artist and find out as much as you can about them. *The Dictionary of Watercolour Artists* may be useful. Many watercolours are not signed, or are only initialed, and may be by a gifted amateur who is impossible to identify.

Staining caused by damp.

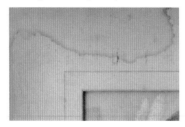

Foxing caused by damp.

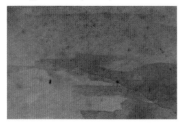

Quality is the next gauge. It is hard to define, but may best be judged as the skill with which the artist grades colour and light. Compare your picture with those by a great watercolourist such as Copley Fielding or Seago (*see right*).

The subject of your picture is significant: landscapes are probably the most common, but not necessarily the most valuable, although identifiable places will have greater value. Seascapes are more popular, and specialist subjects, such as wartime scenes or book illustrations, are avidly collected. Abstract subjects by 20th-century artists such as Ben Nicholson are rare and valuable.

Condition is important in assessing value as watercolours are prone to damage. If left the in sun they fade, and if they become damp they develop mould spots (foxing) or a 'high tide mark' stain. Restoration is expensive and almost never worth doing before selling.

Watercolours can be faked, but only artists at the top end of the market are usually affected, such as Turner or John Piper. If you think you may have an old master, look at reference books on the artist and consult an

WHAT TO LOOK FOR…

Is it signed? A signature will add to the painting's value.

Is it damaged, either faded or foxed? If so, it will diminish value considerably.

Is it framed or just in a mount? It may need remounting before selling but will look 'new' and possibly worth leaving to buyer.

Does the artist have RWS after his name (a member of the Royal Watercolour Society)? If the artist belong to this or another society it will be worth more.

expert or dealer. Popular watercolours, such as Helen Allingham's cottage scenes, were often also issued as prints and can be hard to distinguish unless taken out of the frame. Print paper is shinier and the print will have a 'photographic' quality.

William Earl Johns (1893–1968),
Three Bi-planes Performing Acrobatics.
The subject is very important. WWI subjects are often sought after and planes also have their specialist admirers.
£1,100–1,400

Look at the quality of the **light**, how it is conveyed – will add to its value.

The picture is in good condition with no **staining or spotting**, which adds to value.

The picture is **signed** which increases value doubly so here as the artist is also the well-known author of the Biggles books.

WHAT HAVE YOU GOT?

E. Kuhlbrannott, *A horse and Dog in a landscape*, signed and inscribed, watercolour, late 19thC/20thC.
£50–60

Arthur Suker, *Cumberland Views* (one of a pair), signed, watercolour, 19thC.
£160–190

Thomas Frederick Collier, *Still Life with Pansies*, signed, watercolour, 19thC.
£500–600

Feliks Topolski, *Equestrian Study*, signed, pen and watercolour.
£540–650

Sir Alfred East, *Girl, Geese and Thatched Cottage*, signed, watercolour, 19thC.
£600–700

Ernest Arthur Rowe *Vesuvius and the Bay of Naples from Sorrento*, signed and inscribed, watercolour.
£4,000–5,000

Prints

Prints come in many forms. A variety of techniques are used and, though none is intrinsically more valuable than another, today some are more saleable than others. Artists from Rembrandt and Goya to Picasso and Henry Moore all made prints using a variety of techniques such as engraving, etching, drypoint, screenprinting and lithography, to name but a few.

WHATEVER the technique, a design is created by the artist on a flat surface such as a copper plate, a sheet of paper is pressed down onto it, printing the image onto the paper, a process that can be repeated many times.

The value of many prints is determined by whether or not it is an 'original' print – one that has been produced by the artist – and if the quantity printed has been controlled (limited edition). Look to see if your print has been signed and numbered. It may have, for example, the number 5/40, meaning that this is print number five in an edition of 40. It does not matter where your print comes in the edition (number 30 is as good as number five). A print may exist in several 'states', when the artist alters

the design and then produces another edition.

Older prints before the late 19th century will not be numbered. Some prints continued to be produced from original plates by artists such as Rembrandt, and more recently Thorburn, even though the artists are long dead. Some 19th-century prints, such as hunting scenes by Certes or Jorrocks, are hand-coloured. They are lively and characterful and if you have the full set of four or six it will be much prized.

Look for a watermark in the paper. If you hold it up to the light you may see what looks like a rubber stamp with the makers' name or trademark. This may help confirm that the print is authentic and not a copy or, worse, just a photocopy. If you look carefully you should

<table>
<tr><td>

WHAT TO LOOK FOR...

What technique has been used? Adds to interest rather than value.

If it is a 20th-century print does it have a signature and an edition number? If it is a signed limited edition print it will be worth more.

Does it have a printer's stamp? This will help to confirm the print as being authentic.

Has the margin around the print been cut down or cut out? Reduces the print's value considerably.

Is it one of a set? Is the set complete? A complete set will be worth much more than a single print.

</td></tr>
</table>

also be able to see a plate mark, where the edge of the plate with the design on it has been impressed into the paper during the printing process.

Like any work on paper, prints are prone to damage from damp or rough handling and condition affects price. In addition, if the blank margin round the print has been cut down, this diminishes the value. Beware of prints of birds and flowers in case they have been torn out of books as, with few exceptions, they will be worth little.

Plate mark.

Signature and edition number.

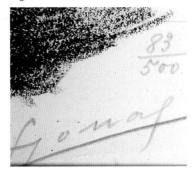

Duck Shooting, *hand-coloured engraving, 19thC.*
One of a set of six prints on different types of shooting.

This is a 19thC print so it will not have a limited edition number which does not diminish its value. If the margin has been cut down or if the print has been cut out of a book, this considerably reduces its value.

Condition is important. Like watercolours, prints may suffer from the damp or fade in sunlight which will diminish its value.

An interesting or attractive **subject** will always add to the value.

This is one of a **set**. Would be worth less if one of the set was missing.

The **name of the artist** and the engraver are engraved onto the plate. Helps if you can identify artist and adds value. May be faked, although generally only great artists' works are faked.

WHAT HAVE YOU GOT?

Cecil Aldin,
Winter Coaching Scene
Known for his humorous subjects, c1910.
£15–20

Charles Rosenberg,
South West View of St Nicholas' Church,
aquatint with hand colouring.
£200–240

William Wyllie,
Thames Barges with St Paul's Cathedral and the Tower of London, one of a pair, etching.
£1,000–1,500

Patrick Caulfield RA,
Spider Plant,
silkscreen print, signed and numbered 69/72.
£300–360

Henry Moore,
Reclining Figure, Cave, lithograph, signed and numbered edition of 50.
£1,500–1,750

Elisabeth Frink,
Man and Horse,
screenprint, signed edition of 70
£3000–3,500

Ceramics

British, Continental, Oriental, Art Nouveau and Art Deco

Every house contains ceramic objects ranging from dinner plates to china figures. How do you tell which are worth selling? Almost no china that is cracked, chipped or stained will have a value unless it is particularly old and rare. However, old rivets may be a sign of a valued object which was worth mending, so do not automatically bin it without consulting an expert.

GENERALLY speaking, weed out the damaged and worn crockery and concentrate your attention on finding out more about those pieces that are ornamental, in good condition and stylish. Decorative items such as vases are generally more popular than practical ones such as plates.

Some ceramics will be marked (you can look these marks up either in reference books or on the internet,) but a great deal is not and you will therefore have to follow the clues given by the shape, subject matter and type of clay body to lead you to an attribution. One useful site to access is www.antiquestradegazette.com (although you will need to subscribe to this website). As a great trading nation, Britain has been importing ceramics from the rest of the world for hundreds of years, so the possible source of your piece could just as well be China, Japan, France or Germany.

In the last five years the market has changed considerably, with the demand for traditional subjects switching to more striking styles such as Art Nouveau and Art Deco. For these quality is less important than style and buyers are looking for good clear colours and shapes that will make an object stand out in a room. That being said, there are a number of collectable areas (*see pp44–45*) that seem to buck the trend, such as the flamboyant Royal Doulton figures, Beswick animals and Hummel figures.

Another improving market is Oriental porcelain. The strength of the Chinese economy has produced a number of Chinese collectors prepared to pay high prices for good Chinese porcelain. Some traditional areas are still buoyant, such as blue and white china. Pattern and type of object, generally the bigger the better, will play an important part in their attractivness to a potential buyer. Old favourites such as Staffordshire figures have dropped in popularity and are now harder to sell.

Most objects will sell better if they look good, so it is worth washing dusty china carefully in warm soapy water before selling. If, however, it is soft earthenware with crazing, do not wet – simply wipe. Be aware that china is susceptible to damage when in transit so always pack it carefully, especially figures with vulnerable limbs. If plates are stacked, layer paper or bubble wrap between them.

English Traditional Porcelain

From the 1740s most British porcelain was 'soft-paste', made to a recipe that did not contain kaolin. It did not compare with the high quality 'hard-paste' porcelain made elsewhere in Europe. By the early 19th century the recipe for bone china – a soft-paste porcelain strengthened with bone ash – was well-known and a number of factories started making wares in this new, durable ceramic.

THE DECORATION on English porcelain can sit under or over the glaze. Some designs were highlighted with gilding. Simple flower sprays and chinoiserie subjects on a white ground are typical motifs, but you will also find animals, country scenes or titled subjects, which may well be worth more.

Condition is important. Look closely at the surface; if the decoration is in poor condition it can affect the value. The value of very rare objects is less affected by damage. If the enamels (colours) were applied over the glaze they may well be worn. This will also apply to gilding. Minimal wear is acceptable, but cracks or crazing of the glaze, causing discolouration, or even undermining the object's structure, greatly reduces the value.

Now look at the base of the piece, it may be marked. Many factories marked their wares and the symbols used can help to identify both the maker and the date of manufacture. However, many factories left their wares unmarked – and the names of many small, short-lived producers have been forgotten – and so it may be impossible to discover who made a particular piece. If there is a mark, look it up in a reference book or research it on the internet.

Values unfortunately have not risen in the last 15 years as understated traditional patterns do not appeal to the current taste for bold designs. However, there are some makers that are still eagerly collected with their values rising, including Swansea and the Welsh factory Nantgarw.

Chelsea anchor mark.

An example of crazing of the glaze.

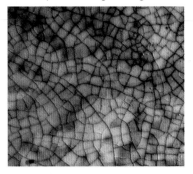

Royal Crown Derby plate, **c1933**
The finely detailed decoration includes flower sprays and gilding surrounding a country scene, which makes the plate more desirable.
£300–350

Look at the **colour** of the porcelain – Bloor Derby 1820–40 is a warm creamy white, whereas Royal Crown Derby is a crisper white with a slight grey tinge.

The **gilded rim** is typical of Derby's plates.

Saucer-like plates, with a more curved rim, were favoured by Derby.

The **blue ground** (the background colour of the rim) with gilding is popular among collectors, making the object more valuable.

The plate may have slightly **warped** in firing, but it was not considered a reject and does not affect value.

WHAT HAVE YOU GOT?

Royal Crown Derby dish, decorated with Japanese pattern. 19thC.
£120–145

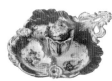

Coalport inkstand with distinctive blue ground, 19thC.
£180–200

Coalport tea set, including sugar bowl and creamer, c1840.
£300–350

Worcester teapot, with characteristic flower spray decoration, c1770.
£450–500

Parian figure entitled *Storm*, c1870.
£540–600

English Traditional Pottery

Pottery made from fired clay is opaque and porcelain is very often translucent. It is not necessarily any thinner than porcelain, in fact thinly potted pottery can indicate high quality. The smooth body (clay) was often covered in a transparent lead glaze and the decoration was hand-painted or transfer printed.

MANY PIECES were decorated either in a naïve English style or with chinoiserie subjects. They tended to be simply made, produced in large quantities and inexpensive. They are often charming but not refined, typified perhaps by brightly-coloured Staffordshire figures.

On English delftware the white clay was covered with a blue-tinted glaze to make a purer white. It was often decorated in blue with designs taken from Chinese porcelain or Dutch examples such as flowers, sometimes in pots, or with exotic birds. Typically it was used to make plates, cups and bowls for the rising middle classes, as were creamware and pearlware.

Some larger manufacturers, such as Wedgwood and Leeds, marked the majority of their output, but many of the smaller potteries such as Liverpool rarely did.

Sunderland lustre, made by several factories from c1790 until the late 19th century, was particularly popular. Fired in a reducing kiln, the enamel is lustrous (like mother-of-pearl) and usually pink, but it can be yellow, black or copper. These wares often combined printed and painted decoration and often commemorated topical events (the Napoleonic wars, Sunderland Bridge) or religious themes, and were sometimes personalized and inscribed accordingly.

The manufacture of tin-glazed earthenware in England began in the late 16th century. Around 90 per cent of English delftware is blue and white, painted in the Chinese style. All tin-glazed earthenware is prone to damage, most notably chips to the rims. This can reduce the value although pieces in perfect condition may be copies, so beware. Antique ceramics have often been repaired with rivets. This may be a good sign as the piece was expensive and treasured (the rivets may be 100 years old). Do not take the rivets out – enjoy them as part of the piece's history.

Because of the high value of rare English pottery there are many fakes, and there are some very convincing modern copies of Staffordshire figures being produced in China.

The market value of English traditional pottery depends on its rarity. Ornamental objects such as vases and figures are more desirable than practical ones such as plates.

WHAT TO LOOK FOR...

Is it pottery or porcelain? Pottery is never translucent.

Does it have a mother-of-pearl sheen? May be Sunderland Lustre.

Is it marked? Factory marks or signatures may improve its value.

Is it chipped or broken? If so, this will reduce value.

Is the piece decorated in red and blue with gilding in a Japanese style? If so, it may be Mason's Ironstone, which will have an impressed mark. The word 'Improved' means it was made after c1840. It has a bluish-grey body which rarely chips, rather it breaks and it may have been riveted.

Mason's Ironstone bowl, **£1,300–1,400**

Staffordshire figure of Shakespeare and muses, c1820.
The triangular compostion of this group is very typical.
£450–550

The **colours** should be good and bright.

Look at the **back**. It is flat and undecorated indicating a poorer quality figure. One moulded and coloured on all sides for display in the round is better quality and more desirable.

Condition is the most important factor – if the object has been **repaired** it will substantially reduce the value.

Look at details such as hands. The quality of the **moulding** is not fine but is typical.

Larger figures, up to 18in (46cm high), are more sought after.

Named figures or groups are much more desirable and valuable.

WHAT HAVE YOU GOT?

Creamware teapot with matching cover, c1770.
£220–260

Spode creamware part dessert service, c1810. A full service is much harder to find.
£250–300

One of a set of four Victorian transfer-printed tiles, in good condition.
£280–330

English delft charger, 18thC.
£360–400

Sunderland lustre wall plaque, c1830.
£370–420

Pearlware coffee pot, in good condition c1790.
£620–680

Continental Porcelain

Much Continental porcelain was expensive at the time. Made from the early 18th century in hard-paste porcelain, it was fired at very high temperatures so that it vitrified, like glass, and became similarly shiny and reflective. Hard-paste porcelain tends to feel colder than the slightly warmer English soft-paste porcelain. Hard-paste porcelain was particularly suited to figures that expressed great movement.

CONTINENTAL PORCELAIN was imported and sold at high prices to the fashion-conscious middle and upper classes. Apart from beautifully detailed figures and figure groups, heavy, highly decorated porcelain tableware was much in demand in the 1860s, as were candelabra, wall plaques and dressing table sets.

There were many Continental manufacturers including Doccia in Italy and Sèvres in France, although the best were probably from Germany, such as Meissen, Ludwigsberg, Frankenthal and Berlin. Pieces from these factories are often marked. Perhaps the most famous mark is the Meissen crossed swords, which changed over time and may be accompanied by a shape number. A good

Meissen mark c1880–1930.

reference book will allow you to date a piece from these marks. Meissen marks are often faked and their figures copied. The fakes will be of lesser quality and usually lighter in weight.

Sèvres is probably Meissen's main competitor. They used a lighter body and employed a more 'feminine' style to produce a softer effect. The factories had a favourite range of colours, peculiar to them, including three blues, a pink and gilding, often with 'jewelled' work alongside it which identifies the factory immediately.

Cheaper bisque figures were also produced in France to satisfy the demand for ornaments. Made in a two-part mould, they are hollow and therefore light. These figures were unglazed and multi-coloured. They were not marked and continued to be made from the 1880s into the 1920s. As they are unglazed they can become dirty, and it may be worth washing them in warm, soapy water.

Russia, too, produced figures, often of peasant children at a daily task such as gathering wood. The Gardner factory was famed for its unglazed figures, which were often of sombre colours, particularly blue. Russian figures are often marked.

Dinner and tea services are often marked with a factory signature and value does depend on this signature. While some services are collectable, others shout quality but do not have a collector's following. The presence of matching serving items such as tureens, meat plates, tea and coffee pots plus the number of plates and bowls can add to the value of the service.

WHAT TO LOOK FOR...

Is it marked? Marks may help to identify the maker but, remember, many marks are fakes..

Is It damaged? Chips and hairline cracks, even though these generally do not discolour, will usually diminish the value of a piece unless it is particularly rare.

Look at the shape – is it bold? German factories are particularly known for their expressive figures and quality of moulding. Proportion and strength of design are important features that add value to a piece.

Test the weight? It should be heavy – in fact, the heavier the better.

Meissen figure of a Girl at a Dressing Table, c1900.
Figures in this style were made at the Meissen factory from the 18thC into the 20thC. Examples from the 18thC are much more valuable.
£600–700

Look at the quality of the detail of the **modelling** – the hands, feet, fingers or jewellery. The greater the detail the better the figure, which will be reflected in the value.

The **solidity** of the figure, the detail of the hair and the confidence of the design all indicate that this figure was made by Meissen.

Look under the base for a **factory mark.** As it is Meissen it should have the crossed swords (*see left*). It also has an **impressed number** which means it must have been produced between 1880 and 1930.

The base is thickly walled, with a broad **foot rim** typical of German figures.

WHAT HAVE YOU GOT?

Conta & Boehme fairing, Germany, c1900.
£30–35

Sèvres *trembleuse* cup and saucer, 1782.
£140–190

Sèvres bisque figural group, c1900.
£165–195

Gardner figural group, Russia, c1880.
£350–420

Ludwisburg figure, 18thC.
£380–450

Limoges part dinner service, late 19thC. The larger the service the more valuable.
£400–450

Blue and White Ceramics

Probably still the most popular of English ceramics, most blue and white pottery is characterized by a cream-coloured earthenware body and blue transfer-printed design. Aimed at an unsophisticated provincial audience, it was made by many factories from 1760 onwards.

BLUE AND WHITE is still being produced, so it is important to establish the age of your piece. Much is not marked so look for signs of ageing that are hard to fake. Characteristic fine crazing can be a good indicator of age and use. Look at the underside for signs of wear on the base. Flatware can have three stilt marks in a triangle on the underside where the piece was propped up in the kiln during glazing. These are not present on modern china.

Blue and white wares were designed for everyday use, so most pieces are functional. Ornamental pieces can be rare and valuable. The design was transfer-printed onto the body and then glazed, protecting the pattern from wear. Some blue and white, such as that by Spode or Rogers, is better quality and is often worth more. It is more likely to be marked if it comes from a bigger factory. Look up any marks in a reference book such as *Miller's Pottery & Porcelain Marks* or Geoffrey Godden's *Encyclopaedia of British Pottery and Porcelain Marks*.

There are many patterns, some with imaginary Oriental scenes, others with English scenery or views with ruins. If rare scenes are titled, such as Minton's views, which have the title and maker's initials painted on the base, they can be more valuable. The rarest patterns such as the Zebra or Elephant command a premium. Look for a pattern in *The Dictionary of Blue and White Printed Pottery 1780–1880* by A. W. Coysh and R. Henrywood. Beware of facsimile china such as by Wood & Son, marked with the original 19th-century print and title.

For collectors, bigger and rarer is generally better. A single plate is most often less desirable than a tureen, serving dish or footbath. An interesting shape in a rare pattern will increase the value considerably. Dinner services complete with meat plates and tureens are rare and valuable. Most blue and white is collected for display rather than use, so some damage is acceptable. If your object is slightly damaged do not get it repaired, sell as is.

Nearly all blue and white transfer-printed wares were made in England. The market in blue and white is steady.

WHAT TO LOOK FOR...

Is it German or French?
Look on the bottom for a mark. Notable factories include Minton, Rogers, Spode and Copeland & Garrett.

Is it a deep, rich blue? Is characteristic of the period 1800–30, while paler blue is generally later.

Is there severe crazing?
This can let in moisture and stain the body, diminishing its value.

Death of the Bear.

Palladian Porch.

Wandering Monk.

English Scenery.

Soup tureen, decorated with Willow pattern, 1830–50.
Tureens are sought after shapes. It also has a good profile and well-pronounced loop handles, making it a desirable object.
£120–140

The **cover** (lid) increases the value significantly, but the tureen would still be very saleable without it.

The Willow pattern is not rare but it is highly collectable.

If it still had its own **ladle or spoon** (which is rare) it would add considerably to its value.

The **thickness** of the potting is a sign of good quality.

The **mellow blue colour** indicates a date of 1830-1850 and is desirable among collectors.

This would be even more collectable if the loop **handles** were shell handles, which can add up to 40 per cent to the value.

It has no **stand** (large under-dish), which reduces its value.

It is unmarked on the base – a notable factory mark would make it more desirable..

WHAT HAVE YOU GOT?

John Richard Riley plate, flower arrangement series, 1800–50.
£150–165

Spode water jug, decorated with a Chinaman of rank, 19thC.
£1,500–1,750

Transfer-printed meat plate, entitled 'Vintage', 19thC, 18½in (47cm) wide.
£3,000–3,500

Staffordshire child's part dinner service, 18thC.
£120–150

Transfer-printed footbath, early 19thC, 16in (40.5cm) wide.
£1,400–1,650

Oriental Ceramics

By the 16th century, Oriental porcelain was in great demand in Europe, causing Western potters to copy it but they did not discover the art of making hard-paste porcelain until the early 1700s, when wealthy Europeans had amassed collections of Oriental wares. Demand continued when European factories made their own porcelain, as the Oriental wares were relatively affordable.

TO ESTABLISH whether a piece of Chinese porcelain has some age look for tell-tale clues, such as when you hold a plate or dish up to the light it may look slightly warped and have a somewhat uneven surface caused by the puddling of the glaze. You may also be able to see and feel the stilt marks where plates were stacked in the kiln. Early pieces are known for their pure white ground and thin, tightly fitting, glassy glaze.

The majority of the Oriental porcelain you will come across will be Chinese rather than Japanese. Huge quantities of Chinese porcelain were imported from 1700 onwards through the Dutch East India Company. Much of it was painted (not printed) in blue

Chinese six-character mark.

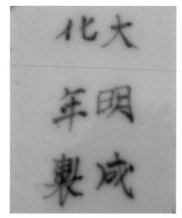

and white, but there is also coloured enamel work such as the famous *famille rose* palette. Traditional flower patterns include chrysanthemum, lotus, peony, and prunus.

Much early Chinese porcelain has a reign mark. A four- or six-character mark (*see below*) was used but, confusingly, of an earlier emperor's reign – not in an attempt to fake the piece but as a mark of respect. This does not affect the value.

Cargos of shipwrecked Dutch East India Company ships, such as the Geldermalsen (known as the Nanking Cargo), which sank in 1752, have been sold in the last 20 years, creating a new collecting area. Shipwreck ceramics are usually tableware, painted in enamels (overglaze colours) or in underglaze blue. Lying for centuries on the sea bed has caused almost total loss of the enamel decoration but the underglaze blue ware has survived in perfect condition. The market for good quality Chinese porcelain is improving with buyers bidding from mainland China.

Good quality Japanese porcelain is equally valuable and often unmarked. Japanese design is more intricate. One of the most famous is the

WHAT TO LOOK FOR...

Is it cold when held to your cheek? If so, then it could be hard-paste porcelain and possibly Chinese.

Test the weight? Some Chinese porcelain is heavier than you would expect.

Can you feel or see marks on either the top or bottom surface, or both? These are marks left by stilts used in the firing process, and are not considered a defect but are a clue that a piece is authentic.

Is the decoration dark blue and red? It may be Japanese Imari pattern but this was copied by many English factories.

Is it chipped on the rim? Not necessarily considered a defect.

Imari pattern made in Japan and exported in large quantities between 1860 and 1930 and therefore commonly found. It is characterized by a dark blue and red palette or sometimes with the addition of yellow and green, often with gilding. Many pieces were purely ornamental and although robust, chips (called fritting) can be found in the glaze on the rim and and are not considered a defect. The glaze may also be pitted.

Chinese export dinner plate, c1740.
This type of Oriental floral pattern was popular in the west, as was the blue and white colour palatte.
£80–85

Stilt marks are a typical feature and may be visible both top and bottom; they can be seen and felt, and do not affect value.

The **glaze** may have puddled – if you allow light to strike it obliquely you may see an uneven surface.

If the glaze is **pitted,** it is a useful identifying feature.

The floral pattern, typical of Oriental ceramics, is **hand-painted** in blue.

The **body** has a bluish tinge, not a creamy one.

WHAT HAVE YOU GOT?

Figure of a bearded Chinese dignitary.
£50–60

Satsuma vase, Japan, late 19thC.
£70–80

Famille rose bowl, China, 1736–95 Popular design with English collectors.
£80–100

Pair of Imari wall plates, Japan late 19thC.
£120–145

Canton baluster vase, China, 1880–1900.
£130–160

Chinese export soup bowl, from Nanking cargo, c1750.
£350–400

Art Nouveau and Art Deco

Art Nouveau was a completely new style employing sinuous, plant-like forms and decoration. It began in France and was popular in Britain until the First World War. As a result of the Paris Exposition des Arts Decoratifs in 1925, Art Deco, with its angular, geometric forms, became fashionable.

MOST ART NOUVEAU ceramics are earthenware and are usually ornamental pieces and teaware. Art Nouveau shapes were used for more expensive items, while the more utilitarian pieces tended to retain traditional shapes but employ Art Nouveau decoration. The Florian pattern Moorcroft vase (*see below*) is typical of the period. Both the decoration and the shape are Art Nouveau. It is marked with a painted signature and Florian mark.

Doulton produced wares that were often upmarket and

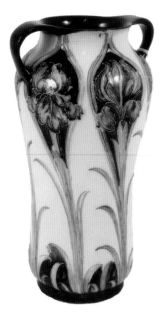

Moorcroft Florian pattern vase. Fine crazing is almost always present but does not reduce value.

expensive, always marked, and sold in department stores. These were decorated with stylized flower, leaf or curling forms, or bear transfer-printed scenes including motoring or literary themes. Nearly all are marked on the base.

Art Deco shapes changed to angular and patterns became more rigid. It was immediately popular and adopted at all levels. Even downmarket makers quickly switched to geometric shapes such as square plates. Upmarket producers such as Wileman & Co produced the Shelley range, mass-produced tableware with the most expensive Art Deco decoration on Art Deco shapes, in bone china. Their wares were always marked. They also produced a cheaper range, with Art Deco designs on traditional shapes.

A number of new designers came to prominence, such as Clarice Cliff at Wilkinsons pottery and Keith Murray at Wedgwood. All Clarice Cliff's designs have a date code impressed into the base.

High quality Continental Art Nouveau and Art Deco porcelain was imported from France, Germany, Austria and Denmark, such as Royal Copenhagen. All of it is

marked. The value depends on the quality of the piece.

Some wear is acceptable, but even expensive pieces are worth little if severely damaged.

The market in these wares is strong, with demand exceeding supply. Always look for quality of design.

WHAT TO LOOK FOR...

Is the style of the decoration reflected in the shape? The best quality pieces have Art Nouveau decoration on an Art Nouveau shape, or Deco on Deco, and are worth more.

Is it marked? Many, such as Doulton Seriesware, are marked.

Does it look like Clarice Cliff? Look for a mark on the base, but beware of fakes.

Is it signed or marked by a well-known designer? For the collector the name of the designer is important. Clarice Cliff, Charlotte Rhead, Susie Cooper and Keith Murray are among the most sought after designers.

Is it damaged? Fine crazing is present on much Art Nouveau and Art Deco pottery and is accepted. Anything more severe will reduce value.

Myott fan vase, 1920–30.
The angular geometric form of this vase is typical of Art Deco wares. Inventive shapes such as the fan and pyramid-shaped objects by Myott, Son & Co are always desirable.
£500–550

These wares were mass-produced, but hand-painted, and they are collectable for **quality of the design**.

Art Deco objects utilized angular **geometric shapes.**

Wacky, **bright colours** are typical of the period – the combination of this particular design and colour is rare.

Myott, Son & Co wares have printed marks under the base.

A **stepped base** can often be found on Art Deco pieces.

WHAT HAVE YOU GOT?

Doulton Seriesware plate, 1920. Some designs are rarer and therefore more valuable.
£40–45

Wedgwood mug, by Keith Murray, 1930s. Keith Murray's work is very collectable.
£40–50

Carlton Ware vase, 1930s. Value is dependent on condition.
£80–100

Minton matching jug and basin set, 1930s.
£120–140

Clarice Cliff Autumn Crocus pattern tea service, c1932.
£140–160

Meissen Saxonia cabaret service, early 20thC. Complete sets command a premium.
£3,000–3,600

Collectable Ceramics

Collectable ceramics are mostly decorative pieces, often small in size, that can be categorized by belonging to a certain group such as royal commemorative ceramics, or being by a particular maker, such as Troika. For many of them, there is a particular range for the collector to look for. Often they are not collected for their quality but for their amusement value or interest.

THE HAND painted natural patterns on Wemyss are instantly recognisable, with collectors being attracted by their immense charm. There is a wide range of objects, all marked. Wemyss is widely collected and has frequently been copied.

Belleek is made from finely moulded thin, white porcelain, and the shape and date when a piece was made are important aspects. Look on the base of the piece for a mark, which will help to date it. Earlier pieces are often more valuable than late. Pieces are often small and ornamental.

Many popular collectable ceramics date from the 1930s to the '80s, and were often produced on a large scale.

Some ranges are huge, such as Royal Doulton figurines, where over 3,000 different models have been made. Prices range from tens of pounds to thousands, depending on rarity.

Other figures that are avidly collected include Beswick animals, and Goebel figures known as 'Hummel' after the name of the nun who designed them; the range is vast.

Commemorative china is collectable but values vary widely. Beware of 'limited edition' ceramics as it is generally only those produced in editions of a few hundred or less that are collectable. Goss is also collectable, with unusual forms, such as aviation or sporting themes, being particularly sought after.

WHAT TO LOOK FOR...

If Wemyss is it damaged? Wemyss soft earthenware is prone to damage, so some flaws are acceptable. Condition determines value.

Do you have a Beswick animal? Cows and horses are popular subjects. Price depends on shape and model number, as well as rarity of colourway.

Is it a Goebel Hummel figurine? The bigger the better, and earlier examples are the most sought after. Condition is very important.

Is it damaged? Do not discard it as a new collector may well start off with a damaged piece and replace it later with a better, more expensive, example.

Pair of ceramic Princess Elizabeth and Princess Margaret mugs, **£175–190**

Goss post box, **£15–20**

Troika Anvil vase, 1970s.
The shapes produced by Troika are all known. Each has a name and some are worth more, depending on rarity.
£500–550

The **textured finish** is typical of wares from Troika.

There is a different **pattern** on each side of the vase.

Some of Troika's **decorators** are better known than others; if this was by a well-known artist it would be worth more.

Earthy colours are typical on these wares. Value is also affected by the pattern and the colours used.

WHAT HAVE YOU GOT?

Royal Doulton Orange Seller figure, 1940–75.
£70–80

Goebel Hummel Little Goat Herder figure, c1970.
£125–140

Belleek cream jug in the shape of a shell with a coral handle. First Period, 1863–90.
£130–155

Wemyss jam pot and cover, painted with roses, c1900.
£350–400

Royal Worcester bowl, signed 'R. Rushton', early 20thC.
£375–425

Beswick model of a Hereford calf, by Arthur Gredington, 1940–57.
£400–480

Glass

Cut, Engraved, Pressed, Coloured, 20th-Century

Today's glass buyers can be roughly divided into two categories: the collector and the user. The collector tends to be interested in only specific examples, while the user wants glass that is both practical and stylish. Any glass that you sell must appeal to one of these two markets.

GLASS OBJECTS – with the exception of 20th-century glass – rarely have a maker's or designer's mark. This can make it harder to differentiate between the ordinary and the exceptional. With clear glass an expert will first look at the tint of the glass itself. This is because early glass tends to be greyish, while glass made after 1870 – which was produced using gas-fired furnaces – became increasingly brilliant.

Style and decoration are more difficult tools to use for assessing date as there have been numerous revivals of historic styles. Victorian revivals of Venetian, rococo and Gothic styles occurred from the 1870s onwards, while Georgian-revival styles became popular during the 1920s and '30s, making it hard for the non-expert to date pieces accurately. Until the 20th century, the shapes for glassware had changed little in hundreds of years.

Individual glasses, unless extremely rare, have little market value, although sets of glasses, particularly of six or more, are usually worth something. Smaller, Victorian liqueur-style glasses are of limited practicality and, with the demise of sherry drinking, they have little value today. Jugs, particularly large ones, are saleable, but small ones less so. Decanters are sought after; however bear in mind that most had stoppers uniquely matched to fit and without them they tend to be worth little.

The boom area among buyers is 20th-century glass, much of it from Scandinavia but also from Italy and the Czech Republic. Innovatory designers have introduced forms and colours that have taken glass (and its prices) into the realms of art rather than just creating utility pieces, although these continued to be made particularly by British glassmakers, held back by the austerities caused by WWII.

Glass is obviously prone to cracks and chips, particularly to rims and feet. It may be possible to 'repair' a chip, depending on where it is and the thickness of the glass, by grinding it down – but get an expert to do it. It is rarely worth repairing a glass object if you are planning to sell it, unless it is Georgian or, for example, the sixth in a set with a minor chip. If it is a good, practical object it will have a value, even if damaged, although value will be decided by the severity of damage and where it is. If it is cracked or riveted bin it!

SHOP WINDOW
Good quality pieces in today's market

Cut glass candlestick, 1770–75.
£250–300

Kosta tankard engraved with marriage scene, Sweden, c1930.
£100–125

René Lalique pressed-glass Rampillion vase, France, c1925.
£800–900

Loetz Papillion vase, Czechoslovakia, c1905.
£750–850

Ruby flash enamelled scent bottle, Bohemia, 1845–60.
£125–150

Per Lütken Suncatcher sculpture, Denmark, 1975.
£300–375

Cut Glass

Cut glass is a very English thing – so much so that it was known abroad as the *façon d'Angleterre*. Made from lead crystal, the cutting was done by hand, using an abrasive wheel that left a distinctive sharp edge to the design. The golden age of cut glass is the Regency period, and the shapes and styles adopted between 1795 and 1825 continue to be made today.

CUT GLASS was always a status symbol, heavy, flashy and eye-catching. Today, however, its qualities are less appreciated. While historic glass will always have a value, much of the rest is of little interest to buyers. Its quality is not reflected in its value.

As a rule of thumb, Regency cutting is often complex but less deep, whereas after the abolition of glass excise duty in 1845 the motifs became simpler but cut much deeper into even heavier glass.

Owing to the technical expertise required to cut the patterns, and because it is now unfashionable, little cut glass is faked. However, because styles were so often revived there can be a fine line between fake and reproduction. The many copies are invariably 'brighter' unless 'old glass' was deliberately used – as when, for example, 18th-century glass was reproduced in the 1920s.

Large amounts of cut glass were imported from the Continent from the mid-19th century onwards. The glass used is not usually lead crystal and therefore weighs less and it does not possess the bell-like 'ping' that is unique to crystal. It is worth less than cut glass made from lead crystal. Busier, fussier pieces of cut glass are less desirable today than plainer ones.

Until the 20th century, few pieces were signed. Bold, modern pieces, perhaps more of a design statement, will sell, as will names such as John Luxton for Stuart Crystal. Many of Luxton's more stylish designs were exported to North America, so its rarity in this country adds to its value. Luxton designs have the maker's name STUART etched into the underside of the base.

Cut glass tot glass, 1920.

WHAT TO LOOK FOR...

Is the cutting sharp and deep? If it is more rounded in profile it may be pressed glass, not cut glass.

What style of decoration? If very fussy may not be worth selling as the style is currently out of fashion.

Is it damaged? If so, where and how badly? Reduces its value.

If damaged, is it worth getting it ground down and repaired? The repair process risks destroying the aesthetic balance of the piece if too much glass is removed during restoration. Not worth doing unless the object has sentimental value. The larger/deeper the chip the more expensive it is to restore.

Is the piece useable? If it has a practical purpose, such as a jug or a decanter, it will be more saleable than a solely decorative piece.

Is it dirty? Clean with warm soapy water or, if stained, with denture cleaner. Cloudy whiteness caused by calcium from hard water entering the surface of the glass is very difficult to remove without professional cleaning.

Cut-glass decanter, c1878.
The shape or form will affect the value. A stylish, not over-complicated, shape will be more valuable. Flick it lightly with your finger. If it does not give a bell-like 'ping' it is not crystal and is worth less.
£200–250

Damage to the **rim** is very common and will decrease the value, though it may be possible to polish out a chip.

Hollow diamonds on the neck are a revival of 1740 style of cutting. This is a sign of quality.

Look at the **brilliance** of the glass. Brilliancy increased from 1870 and may help to date the piece.

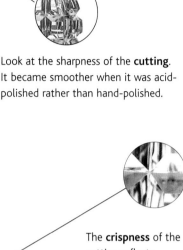

Look at the sharpness of the **cutting**. It became smoother when it was acid-polished rather than hand-polished.

The **crispness** of the cutting reflects improving technology. This is the peak of glass cutting.

The **base** is easily chipped with use and is often damaged. This will reduce value.

WHAT HAVE YOU GOT?

Thistle glass, Scotland, Edinburgh, c1950.
£15–20

Regency-revival cut-glass jug, probably Czechoslovakia, c1925.
£50–60

Regency cut-glass sugar bowl, c1810.
£100–125

Cut-glass covered preserve dish and stand, c1845.
£100–125

Art Deco cut-crystal vase, 1950s.
£120–150

Thomas Webb & Sons cut-glass decanter, c1878.
£200–250

Engraved and Etched Glass

Engraving on glass (as shown here)was an extremely skilled technique. Using a revolving copper disc covered in an abrasive, a design was engraved into the surface of the glass, which in England was usually lead crystal.

THE ENGRAVING has a matt finish and can be used to create extraordinarily fine patterns. Ferns are one of the most common motifs as they were easy to execute. The value now is less than it would have been at the original time of sale: a good quality object is better held onto than sold in today's market. There was a renaissance of engraving in Sweden between 1920 and the 1950s, most notably by Orrefors, mosts of whose pieces are signed (*see below*). Many designs are easily found and therefore worth little.

Acid etching may be regarded as the poor man's engraving. Originally used to decorate glass for pub windows, it was applied to glasses and tableware from around 1865 onwards. Some is of very good quality, and it can be hard to tell the difference between acid etching and engraving. The design was etched with a needle before being dipped in acid, so it is minutely proud of the surface – if you run your thumbnail over it you will feel that it is slightly raised. A typical feature on acid-etched items is a small curly border (*see below*) that cannot be easily achieved with engraving. Today, there is not much difference in value

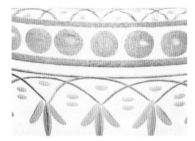
Engraved border.

Acid etched border.

between engraved and acid-etched glass.

Acid paste was also used to create patterns on glass, but is of poor quality. It was cheap and much used, for example, by hotels and railway companies. It tends to be utilitarian and not worth much. Sandblasting was used at many glassworks, including Kosta from the 1930s and Wedgwood and Caithness in the 1970s and is sought after.

Engraved Örrefors signature.

Etched signature.

Engraved glass, c1870.
Complexity of the pattern (*see right*) is a sign of quality. The best designs are figurative, then geometric – like this example – and finally floral.
£65–75

Etched decanter, c1880.
The decanter will, as a practical object, be more sought after than a single glass.
£220–250

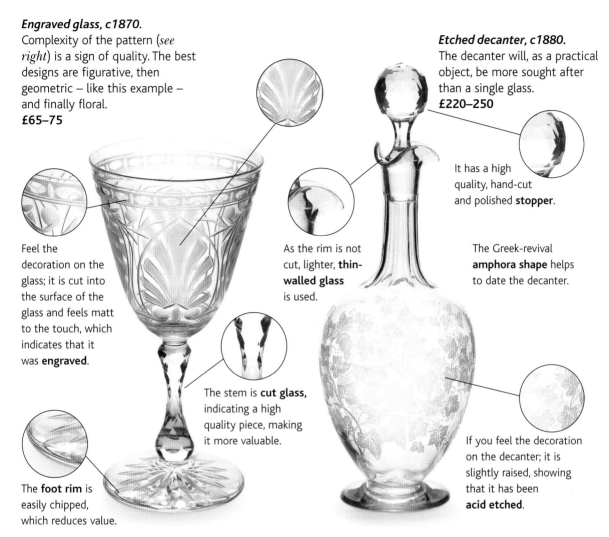

It has a high quality, hand-cut and polished **stopper**.

Feel the decoration on the glass; it is cut into the surface of the glass and feels matt to the touch, which indicates that it was **engraved**.

As the rim is not cut, lighter, **thin-walled glass** is used.

The Greek-revival **amphora shape** helps to date the decanter.

The stem is **cut glass**, indicating a high quality piece, making it more valuable.

The **foot rim** is easily chipped, which reduces value.

If you feel the decoration on the decanter; it is slightly raised, showing that it has been **acid etched**.

WHAT HAVE YOU GOT?

Acid-etched Champagne coupe, 1900–10.
£5–10

Kosta vase, engraved with horse's head Sweden c1959.
£65–75

Goblet, engraved with ferns, in good condition, c1870.
£65–75

Kosta sandblasted vase by Tyra Lundgren, Sweden, c1930.
£80–100

Jug and goblet, engraved with ferns, probably Scottish, c1880.
£250–300

Ercole Barovier acid-etched bowl, Italy, Murano, c1950.
£1,000–1,250

Pressed and Moulded Glass

Some of the earliest Roman vessel glass was moulded, and in more recent times the legal requirement for standard sizes drove the use of high-quality blown moulding. The molten glass was blown into a mould and turned, leaving no mould seam.

THE MOULDS were formed in two or more sections, according to the complexity of the design. Until about 1810, pieces were mould-blown plain and decorated afterwards. Later on, decorated moulds were used. If a design was to be transferred onto the glass, then the molten glass could not be turned within the mould, so there is always a visible seam where the parts of the mould were joined. Unlike cut glass, mould-decorated glass has smoother, softer lines. If you are uncertain whether

Pressed or moulded glass can be identified by the mould seam.

or not a piece has been mould-decorated or pressed (*see below*), run your finger up the inside; you will be able to feel where the glass has bulged out to fill the mould. Most mould-decorated objects will be worth somewhat less than a blown one with the decoration added later on.

Pressed glass, as the name implies, was pressed into a mould and has seams that immediately identify it. Simple utilitarian shapes, such as tumblers, were easy to press and their makers did not bother to polish off the seams. Rims were fire-polished and are often irregular. It was made to replicate more expensive glass but is often crude and much of it is of little value. Glass for the masses was produced in varying qualities by an industry which made literally millions of pieces annually.

Pressed glass was made to replicate more expensive glass but is often crude. Although pressed glass tends to be thick and generally unsophisticated, it lends itself to good practical shapes and, once formed, can be cut or gilded, as with Czechoslovakian examples. There are some rare and valuable pieces of pressed glass so do not automatically

WHAT TO LOOK FOR...

Does the object have a mould seam? This means it must be either mould-decorated or pressed glass.

Does the decoration have rounded rather than sharp edges? This indicates mould-decorated or pressed glass.

Are there imperfections in the glass? Contaminants within the glass are a feature of pressed glass and do not decrease the value.

Is there what looks like a hair in the base? This is where the molten glass was snipped off during manufacture and is a feature, not a flaw.

Is the rim irregular? If it is pressed glass it would have been fire-polished by hand. This does not diminish the value.

Is it coloured? Coloured 19th-century pressed glass is much rarer and consequently more valuable.

Is is damaged? Unless a rare object, it will dimish value.

dismiss it as valueless. Remember, most Lalique glass was and still is pressed-glass, and Lalique is much sought after in today's market.

Pressed glass lion c1870.

Taken from the designs for giant bronze lions by Landseer placed at the foot of Nelson's Column, Trafalgar Square. This association adds considerably to its value. Souvenirs like this were often produced in pressed glass, often in differing sizes. Value is often based on association, as here.

£450–500

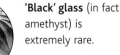

'Black' glass (in fact amethyst) is extremely rare.

The **gilding** is a rare feature. It adds to value as most versions are ungilded.

It is **stamped** with the maker's mark and design patent under the base.

Because of its rarity, the **chip** on the base does not significantly reduce its value.

The **'seam'** shows that it is made of pressed glass.

WHAT HAVE YOU GOT?

Pressed glass Champagne flute, 1860–70.
£15–20

Thomas Webb & Son optic moulded tumbler, c1930.
£15–20

Edward Moore jug, Sunderland, c1850.
£25–30

Nemo series vase, Czechoslovakia, c1950.
£50–60

Marc Lalique, pressed-glass vase, 'Les Moineaux', French, c1940.
£250–300

John Derbyshire pressed glass souvenir lion, c1870.
£450–500

Coloured Glass

The difficulty of producing glassware that had a consistent colour meant that coloured glass was always expensive and therefore a luxury. Much coloured glass was produced in France, Belgium, Germany and Czechoslovakia. As with most forms of glass, signed examples are rare, leaving style and colour as the principal means of identification.

Bohemian gilded and enamelled vase.

THE WAS fierce competition to create new colours and effects, such as French opaline glass, a cloudy effect gained by adding bone ash. Combined with ormolu (gilded brass), it was used to create richly decorative objects, some worth thousands today.

Casing – where two 'layers' of glass are combined, with one colour cut through to reveal the under layer – was popular from the late 19th century. Glass can also be enamelled, often with a pattern, or combined with gilding to create a luxurious effect.

Drinking glasses were usually colourless, mostly because drinks tend to look unpalatable in coloured glass, whereas decorative items such as vases were often coloured.

Coloured glass is still popular today and sells better than colourless equivalents, with red and blue most in demand and amber less so. Fashions in coloured glass have changed. Amber was popular in the 1930s, smoked tints during the 1950s and '60s. Amber is now unpopular, while demand for smoked is rising.

Antique coloured glass is now reproduced in China with a negative effect on the market. For example, the value of Victorian cranberry glass has fallen as even professionals find it difficult to distinguish old from new. The same is also true of so-called 'Mary Gregory' designs, characterized by white enamel figures painted onto a green, blue or cranberry ground.

Casing is a technique where two layers of glass of different colours were used, and the top layer was then cut to reveal the under layer. Although this bowl dates from c1860 it looks surprisingly modern.

Cranberry bowl, c1880.
An example of casing, with a layer of cranberry overlaying clear glass.
A luxury object and therefore valuable. On a cranberry glass object any
handles, feet or stoppers are almost always clear. A 'practical' object in
that it can be used but also a stylish piece, making it appealing to buyers.
£70–80

The **rim** is
unchipped.
Cranberry is a
very strong colour,
the bowl is 90 per
cent colourless
and 10 per cent
cranberry, so
therefore any chip
would be very
obvious and
difficult to repair.

Thick, **heavy, lead crystal**
is a sign of quality.

The bowl is cut
to reveal the
under layer.
Makes it a more
luxurious object
and therefore
more valuable.

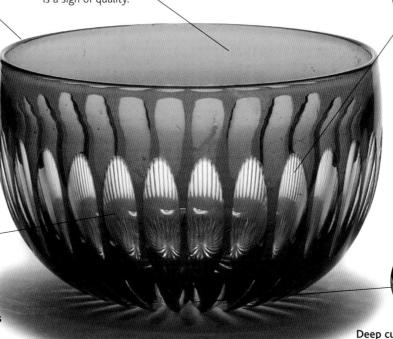

Ovals, known as **lens
cutting**. They are a
sign of quality.

Deep cutting of the
base is a sign of quality.

WHAT HAVE YOU GOT?

Green roemer,
Bohemia,
c1900.
£5–10

Blue pressed-
glass tumbler,
Bohemia,
c1880.
£30–35

Ruby-flash
enamelled scent
bottle, Bohemia,
1845–60.
£125–150

Jug, possibly
Sowerby,
c1880.
£200–250

Clichy spangled
carafe,
France,
c1860.
£250–275

Freeformed
elephant, Italy,
Murano,
1960–70.
£250–300

20th-Century Glass

If you have some 20th-century glass you could be on to a winner. This area of glass collecting is booming, with some pieces increasing in value by as much as 300 per cent in five years.

THE 20TH CENTURY was a period of huge technical innovation, the role of the designer becoming increasingly important. Beginning with Lalique after WWI, a whole new gallery of shapes, colours and textures appeared in glass. After 1945, designs became increasingly idiosyncratic, with use of texture and vivid colours. Glass moved out of the cabinet and assumed a starring role as a design/taste statement. Single dramatic pieces radiate in our well-lit 21st-century homes, so the more dynamic and striking your glass, the greater its value is likely to be.

Examples by well known and respected designers command premiums, particularly for signed examples of their work,

irrespective of their nationality. Much 20th-century glass is collected by designer, but there is a pecking order of popularity, with pieces by the Finnish Tapio Wirkkala, for example, and Italians Dino Martens and Ercole Barovier commanding premiums.

One of the great advantages of 20th-century glass is that much of it is signed. US trade regulations revised in the 1920s meant that all glass had to be marked, not only with its place of origin, but often with its maker's name. Logos were sometimes incorporated into the moulds or applied in acid, but Murano and Sweden tended towards stickers, which were often removed.

Designs were widely plagiarized, so it can be

difficult to attribute a piece confidently. A vibrant market for 20th-century glass has been rapidly developing on the internet, particularly for Whitefriars, although many pieces are mis-attributed. Prices are volatile. Fakes are unusual but there are a few instances of reusing old moulds, such as Geoffrey Baxter's 1966 Drunken Bricklayer vases which, although signed by their new maker, have caused the price of the originals to fall. Try to research a piece on the internet, in a reference book or sale catalogue. Similar examples should help you to value it.

WHAT TO LOOK FOR...

Is it signed? Look for a signature under the base.

Is it a big, bold design? It will often be worth more.

Is it interestingly textured? Textured effects are typical of mid-20th-century glass.

What colour is it? The colour may help you date it – for example, orange is a very 1960s colour. Some colours are more popular.

Is it damaged? A small chip to the base will probably not reduce the value much – however, more serious damage will reduce its worth.

Sommerso bowl, Italy, Murano, 1960–1970, **£100–200.**

Banjo vase, Whitefriars, c1966.
Big, bold design – popular in today's market. Completely new shapes introduced in mid-20thC. Looks good as display objects. Much in demand.
£1,200–1,400

Idiosyncratic form not related to functionality; glass as a design statement.

Innovative use of **texture**, following Scandinavian Finlandia style.

Distinctive **Whitefriars 'pewter'** colour rare. This will increase the value.

Good quality **thick, heavy** glass.

Mould blown and formed in a two-part mould. There is a prominent seam round the diameter.

WHAT HAVE YOU GOT?

Bagley pressed-glass Bedford vase, c1930.
£20–30

Örrefors tumbler, Sweden, c1933.
£25–35

Sommerso vase, Italy, Murano, 1950–60.
£60–75

Per Lütken Aristocrat decanter, Denmark, c1956.
£125–150

Vicke Lindstrand Graal Winter vase, damaged, Sweden, c1954.
£180–200

Nanny Still mould-blown Quadrifolia vase, Finland, c1960.
£200–250

Toys and Dolls

Die-cast Vehicles, Trains, Lead Figures, Dolls, Teddy Bears

Toy collectors are most excited when they find items still in mint condition. Given that so many toys and dolls were manufactured and imported from Victorian times onwards, it is only the exceptions – the ones that were not played with, kept untouched in their original boxes – or of very high quality produced in limited numbers – that fetch big money. Rarity and condition are the most important factors in determining value.

Die-cast toys have been made in considerable quantities for over a century. In the 1960s one British manufacturer alone produced 770 million metal toys in seven years. There are many of them still around and it might seem surprising that any of them are worth very much – but some are worth a great deal. There is a buoyant market, partly fuelled by increasingly international internet sales, particularly in road vehicles.

Similarly, there are any number of teddy bears around and you need to work out if yours is special. Some of them will have a metal button or fabric label that will help you to research them further. There are many reference books but the best remains *The Teddy Bear Encyclopedia* by **Pauline Cockrill** et al. Even more modern bears, like Paddington, can be collectable. The market for soft toys is less buoyant than that for bears, but if in good condition makes such as Chiltern and Farnell are very collectable.

Some bisque and composition dolls were mass produced such as AM A390. It was not until the 1950s that soft plastic dolls were made in a huge numbers. There is considerable interest in the early Barbies and Sindys and their wardrobes, though these early models may suffer from the instability of the plastic resulting in discolouration or, worse, 'plastic melt'. Pre-1950s die-cast vehicles can suffer metal fatigue as a result of impurities in the zinc alloy.

Since some toys and dolls are now worth considerable amounts, restoration and how far it should go have become a problem. Many die-cast toys have been restored, some of them so well done that it is easy to be misled into thinking they are original mint examples. So when is a perfect restoration classed as a fake? When it is passed off as an original.

There are similar problems with bisque dolls, for whom such convincing reproduction heads and limbs have been produced that they have fooled even the experts. If a doll has been kept in a loft or garage for many years it may well have deteriorated beyond repair. Glazes and composition bodies crack, fabrics turn to dust and rubber decomposes. Any marks on the doll will count against you: teeth marks, scratches, wear and tear will all diminish value and, with plastic dolls, marks such as biro are impossible to get out.

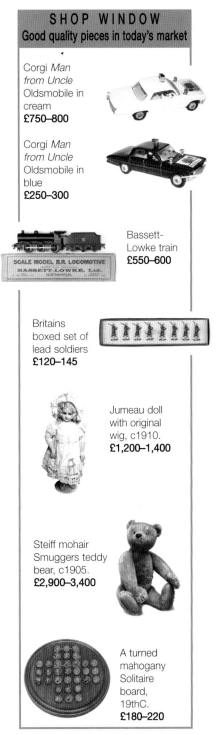

SHOP WINDOW
Good quality pieces in today's market

Corgi *Man from Uncle* Oldsmobile in cream
£750–800

Corgi *Man from Uncle* Oldsmobile in blue
£250–300

Bassett-Lowke train
£550–600

Britains boxed set of lead soldiers
£120–145

Jumeau doll with original wig, c1910.
£1,200–1,400

Steiff mohair Smuggers teddy bear, c1905.
£2,900–3,400

A turned mahogany Solitaire board, 19thC.
£180–220

Die-Cast Vehicles

Perhaps the most famous name in toy cars is Dinky. Early Dinky toy cars are divided into two main periods: pre- and post-WWII, and the date makes a considerable difference to what they may be worth. Matchbox and Corgi, Dinky's main rivals, also have a loyal following among collectors.

WITH DINKY the main features to look at are, firstly, the wheels. If they are pre-war, they will be domed and completely smooth; post-war, the wheels have a rim. Next, look at the axles: pre-war axles are thin, whereas post-war they are thick. Finally, the chassis plate will be open if pre-war and enclosed if post-war. If the car has *all three* period features, it can confidently be dated and valued accordingly. A pre-war car can be worth considerably more than a post-war, apparently identical, version.

The colour is also important. If a model was usually made in a particular colour, say green, then a yellow version (perhaps a special order) or a two-colour edition for export (perhaps to the USA) would be rarer and therefore more valuable.

Until 1947 Dinky toys were not individually boxed, but came in trade boxes usually of six vehicles supplied to retail outlets. Thereafter, first larger

Dinky Toys Jaguar Mark X, early 1960s.

vehicles and then smaller were individually boxed. Boxes in good condition are rare and are themselves quite valuable, so having the original box can double the value of the vehicle. There are modern facsimilie boxes available, generally simply for display purposes.

With Matchbox, the particular make, colour and wheel variations are what will most affect the value. Corgi toys have more features than Dinky, such as opening doors, suspension and were the first to use windows; they also pioneered the link with films and television shows. Both Corgi (*James Bond*) and Dinky (*Thunderbirds*) made hugely successful tie-ins. If these models have their original boxes, especially with the display insert, they are sought after and can be worth five times as much as an unboxed example. They are collectable up to the 1970s. More recent examples are still too widely available to have much value... yet.

The condition of the model is all important. Collectors are attracted by something in mint condition. A vehicle with chipped paint can be worth two-thirds less than a 'factory fresh' vehicle for which a premium price can be made.

WHAT TO LOOK FOR...

What date is it? Whether it is pre- or post-WWII makes a difference to value.

Has the paint has been chipped or a wheel or other part been lost? Will be worth much less.

Has it been repainted? Look for traces of paint where there should be no paint, such as on the base. Repainting lowers the value.

Has any part, such as the radiator, been replaced? This will reduce the value.

Does it have its original box in good condition? Greatly increases the value.

Is it suffering from metal fatigue? In pre-WWII models look for cracks or bulging in the metal.

If models are only lightly chipped or of a rare type, it is best not to have them restored. Most toys are better sold unrestored. Unless it is pre-war (in which case leave it to an expert), it may be worth cleaning the model carefully with a worn, soft toothbrush, warm water and washing up liquid and dry with a soft cloth to bring up the shine on the paintwork.

Dinky Toys truck, 1930s.
Vehicles from this period are rare but survive well as they were made of lead rather than mazac and so do not suffer from metal fatigue, as later post-WWII models do. Later examples also had wheel hubs with white rubber tyres.
£200–220

Colour is typical for this model. Rarer colours are more sought after.

In good **condition**. As it is made of lead there is no metal fatigue but it can bend.

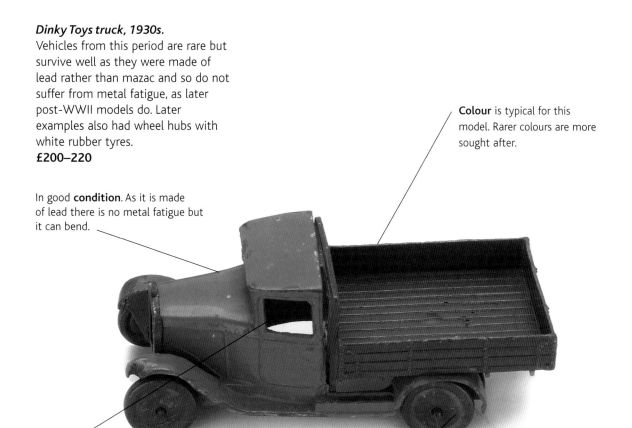

No models of this date have 'glass' **windows**.

Smooth **wheels** show that this is an early pre-WWII model before the introduction of rubber tyres. Ridged, domed wheels would indicate a post-war date.

WHAT HAVE YOU GOT?

Matchbox Yesteryear Steamroller, with original second type box, 1960s.
£15–20

Matchbox American Plymouth car, with original box, 1950s/early 1960s.
£65–75

Triang Spot-On Routemaster London Bus, 1960s.
£225–250

Dinky Toys Joe 90 car, original display, rare example with rear engine cover, late 1960s.
£275–300

Corgi Batmobile, first type in display box, 1960s.
£275–325

Trains

Model trains still exercise a fascination in the male imagination, as proved by the continuing success of Hornby trains. Tinplate and die-cast trains from the mid-1920s to the 1980s have a dedicated band of collectors, and the market is just as international and buoyant as the toy car market.

THE NAME of the maker will affect the value of your train. Look for the manufacturer's label on the cab. Hornby, Triang, Wrenn and Chad Valley always concentrated on the mass-market, whereas Bassett-Lowke were more concerned with quality. Less well known, but not less valuable, is Bowman, which specialized more in live steam.

Model trains come in many gauges: the two most popular are 0 and 00. Dating from the late 1920s through the 1950s, 0 gauge is larger; the narrower 00 gauge was introduced by Hornby in the 1930s as the 'Dublo' range. The other, larger gauges, often for tinplate clockwork trains, comprise the top ten per cent of the market and are often expensive. The larger the locomotive, the more appealing to collectors.

The type of locomotive is important: the number of wheels (expressed as 0-4-0 for four wheels, 4-4-0 for four

smaller and four larger ones, etc) will determine how much it is worth. The company livery, such as Great Western or LNER, is also important as some are more prized than others and there may be local loyalties to a particular company.

Continental manufacturers such as Bing, Märklin and Carrette made good quality, expensive trains for the UK market in 0-, 1- and 2-inch gauges. These are much sought after if in good condition.

A well restored train may look to be in original mint condition. Only an expert will be able to tell. Clockwork trains may have been 'updated' by being converted to take an electric motor, which affects value. Collectors prefer a working train and it may be worth replacing a non-working motor as long as it done by an expert and replaced with the right engine. A certain amount of wear is acceptable, but the price goes down with chipped paint.

Horby 1950s coaches are fairly common, but are collectable.

1920s four-wheeled wagon; in good condition is rare and valuable.

WHAT TO LOOK FOR...

Who was the maker? The name of the maker will affect the value.

Is it part of a set? Boxed sets in good condition command a premium.

What gauge is it? Larger gauges are often worth more.

Is it clockwork or electric? Electric may be worth more.

Converted from clockwork to electric? Look for a winding hole. Reduces value.

If electric, is the motor worn out? Working models are preferred. A replaced motor can be acceptable if it was replaced with the right type.

Is there metal fatigue in the wheels? This is common and accepted but affects value.

Is it complete: does it have its tender if the model requires it? This affects value.

Is the paint chipped and worn? Affects value.

Are there any missing parts? Links, couplings or connecting rods may be missing.

Was the body repainted? Restoration is fine if not being passed off as a mint original.

Hornby 0 gauge 4-4-0 electric locomotive and tender, No. 4, 'Eton', two wheels damaged, late 1930s.
Look at the bodywork to make sure it has not been converted from clockwork and that all parts are original.
£2,200–2,500

Company name should be screen-printed on. If a transfer has been replaced more recently it affects value.

The Southern **livery** is in good condition – adds to value.

Paint not chipped and worn. General wear and tear will reduce the value.

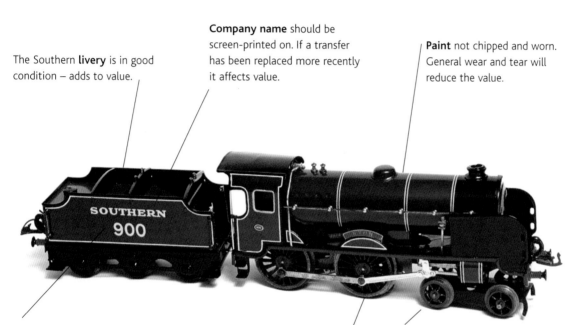

Has its **tender**. If the tender is missing it will reduce the value.

The **wheels** should not be too worn or suffer from metal fatigue – much reduces value.

The **number of wheels** affects the value – this tender engine is worth more than an 0-4-0 engine.

WHAT HAVE YOU GOT?

Hornby 0-4-0 tank engine, 1950s. Fairly commonly found.
£120–140

Hornby clockwork 4-4-0 tender locomotive, (tender not shown) 1930s.
£400–450

Hornby 4-4-4 tank engine, early 1930s. Rare in such good condition.
£400–480

Bing 4-4-2 tank engine, 1920s. Look for cracking (reticulation) on the paintwork.
£300–360

Basset-Lowke 4-6-0 tender locomotive, 1950s, (tender not shown). Rolls-Royce quality.
£750–900

Lead Figures

One of the most popular figure manufacturers is Britains who, between 1890 and 1960, produced most of their figures in lead. All figures made during this period have a value unless damaged. During the late 1960s figures began to be made in plastic and some are now very collectable, despite their now distinctive chemical smell. Figures produced as 'collectables' rather than toys have little value as too many survive.

MANY PEOPLE would have collected Britains toys when young, most typically soldiers. Britains exported toys all over the world. Some of the rarest and most valuable are issues of Continental regiments and representations of, for example, Argentinian soldiers. Other rarer subjects include Boy Scouts and the Salvation Army. Their desirability is linked to production numbers – rarity and value go hand in hand.

Toy figures were hand-painted and some of the painting was fairly crude. At the opposite end of the spectrum were the 'super detailed' special orders, which

1920s–50s farm series are collectable.

are worth considerably more. Some figures will have been repainted, and it can be hard to tell. It takes an expert to spot a feature such as a moustache that should not be there, to determine if the paint is original or a later addition.

Boxed sets are worth at least twice, if not three times, as much as the same figures loose. The condition of the box is important in determining value. Early boxes are much sought after, such as those designed by Fred Whistok and dating from the 1920s. The most valued figures are those still in mint condition in their boxes, tied onto the original backing board with the original string.

Farm and zoo sets were very popular and are still sought after today, particularly those made by Britains. They changed from lead to plastic in the late 1960s but were changed back to a safer metal alloy in the 1970s when they were retailed as 'collectables' rather then toys.

Loose models that have been damaged, for example with a broken limb, are more or less worthless. Obvious repairs, such as the head re-mounted on a matchstick, are not good

news. Restoration is only worthwhile for rare models, but it will still diminish the value. Generally it is better not to restore – leave it to the buyer.

You may have lead figures by a Continental manufacturer such as Heyde, or you might have slightly larger composition (formed over a wire frame) figures by Elastolin and Lineol, which were imported in large quantities. The value of these is largely dependent on subject and condition.

Britains Zoo set, 1950s.
Sets are rare and were made mostly for export to the USA.
£250–300

Is it **complete**?
Worth much
more if it is.

Because the **box**
is very rare it is
still worth
hundreds of
pounds even in
this conditiion.

If figures are tied in with **original stringing**
adds greatly to value.

The pieces are all in **mint condition**. Any broken
legs reduce the value considerably.

WHAT HAVE YOU GOT?

Loose figures in
battered condition
have little value or
casting value to a
restorer.
£10–20

Loose figures in good
condition (six in all),
round base examples
are early,
1900s.
£50–60

Britains Household Cavalry,
12 pieces (gun team shown)
no box,
1950s.
£300–350

Boxed set of Boy Scouts,
a rare and unusual set so
seldom seen, especially in
mint boxed condition.
1950s.
£400–500

China and Composition Dolls

Bisque (or china) dolls were made from 1830 onwards, but most date from 1880 to 1930. They tend to be German or French. Bru, Steiner and Jumeau made top quality dolls: they were not mass-produced and are rare. The most commonly found dolls are made by AM (Armand Marseille) and SFBJ and have an impressed mark on the back of the head and a mould-size number.

ALL CHINA dolls are rare and may date from 1700 onwards. They are smaller than composition dolls, about 9 inches (23cm) high, and are not jointed – they just swing from the shoulder and hip.

Bisque heads came in a number of qualities, with the best having well modelled and finely drawn features (*see below*). They were attached to a number of different bodies: a mix of composition, cloth and hide, hide or kid (made until the 1900s) and rag bodies with composition hands and feet for the cheaper end of the market. These were also used for 'boudoir' dolls, because as they were floppy could 'sit'.

Bru doll with finely painted features.

Composition bodies, made of fibre and glue (similar to papier mâché), are lighter and less cold to the touch than china. They are covered in a glazed coating, which may craze if exposed to temperature changes, such as if stored in a loft. Some crazing is acceptable, but cracks, snapped-off fingers or chipped toes are not a good sign. Even if repaired they reduce the value.

The bisque head and limbs are held together with elasticated stringing. You can gently lift off the head to look inside. This is important to establish that the head is genuine and not a replacement. Using modern materials, modern bisque heads are made from moulds taken from the original – they are correct in every detail, including any marks. The only way to tell is to look inside. You should see where, over time, dirt and dust has seeped in through the mouth and eyes, no matter how well kept. If it is clean and new then it could be a replica. At the same time shine a torch inside to check for cracks – these lower the value.

If the limbs are wonky, it is usually because the old elastic stringing has perished. It may be worth getting it re-strung

WHAT TO LOOK FOR...

Is the head, including the wig, original? Very important for value. Gently lift the head and look inside with a torch for signs of dust and age.

Is the head stamped? Adds to value

Is the doll damaged? Cracks in the head or crazing on the body reduce value as do broken fingers and toes

Is the body jointed? If so it will be worth more than fixed limbs.

If dressed is the clothing original? The original clothes are not documented and would by now probably be browned and distressed, or become hard and crispy. Clothes in this state do not add to the value.

before selling, but ensure that it is properly done, as there is a danger of damage, such as chipped joints. Consult a dealer or auction house.

Dolls with composition heads and bodies were made from the 1930s until plastic took over after WWII. B & D and Pedigree are the most usual makes; both stamped the head or body. Heavy dolls with composite heads and hard plastic bodies were made into the 1950s.

Armand Marseille 390 doll, c1915.
This doll has the AM stamp
on the back of the head.
£200–250

Look at the quality of the
head – including the wig.
Damage to the head
reduces value.

If **joints are loose** it may be
worth tightening them by
getting the doll re-strung.

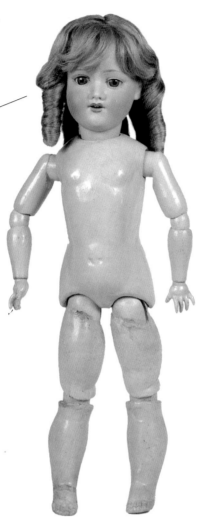

Has it got a **stamp** on
the upper back or
back of the head?
Adds to value.

Is there **cracking or
crazing** on the body?
Reduces value.

Limbs – look for damage
to digits. Reduces value.

How is the body made –
is it **jointed or fixed limb**?
The more sophisticated
the better.

WHAT HAVE YOU GOT?

Rosebud
composition doll,
cloth body and
articulated arms,
America, 1930s.
£115–130

Pedigree hard
plastic doll, bent
knee walking doll
with original wig,
1950s.
£120–140

SFBJ bisque-
headed
composition doll,
No. 236 with
jointed body,
France, 1930.
£160–200

Wax-headed doll
with cloth body,
1830–60.
£200–240

Ideal 'Deanna
Durbin' composition
doll with socket
head and human
hair wig, original
dress, c1940.
£650–780

Bru bisque fashion
doll with swivel
neck on a
gusseted kid
body, France,
c1875.
£3,000–3,200

Plastic Dolls

By the late 1950s vinyl, or soft plastic, had arrived. You can distinguish vinyl from hard plastic as it is squeezy and soft. The most prolific maker of dolls in the UK was Pedigree, the manufacturer of Rosebud and Sindy, the latter produced in response to Barbie, made by the American firm Mattel.

PEDIGREE'S Rosebud doll has a circular mark surrounded by rosebuds. Rosebuds were jointed with elasticated stringing which if loose but not frayed can be tightened. It is easy to get these dolls restrung, but collectors may prefer them in their original state. The market for Rosebuds has been static for 20 years.

Mattel's Barbie arrived in Britain in the 1959s. There were six versions of the same doll – for example, Bubblecut No. 3, referring to her hairstyle. The pearl stud earrings on early Barbies eroded in a damp atmosphere and gave her green ears, causing a drop in value. However, many models are highly collectable.

Sindy was made in 1962 to

Outfits in their original packaging can be valuable.

rival Barbie. The first 12in (30cm) Sindy came in a box and had a single 'weekender' outfit. She had several hair colours, and two head versions: a smaller, harder one made in Hong Kong and a softer, larger version made in Britain; both are stamped on the shoulder. In 1964 Paul was introduced with two hairstyles, one 'hair' the other moulded. The moulded version is worth slightly less. His Beatles outfit is very collectable.

Ideal produced a rival to Sindy called Tammy and her sister Pepper; both are highly collectable, especially in their original boxes. Palitoy's Pippa, only 6in (15cm) high, has multiple hair colours and styles, and accessories for her or her boyfriend, Pete.

Gabriel's Mary Quant doll of the 1960s has a high-fashion wardrobe that is sought after. A doll with its box is worth more.

Action Man prices have fallen sharply as a result of the reissue of the original Action Man. Early Action Man figures are still desirable and early outfits and accessories particularly valuable. The same applies to *Star Wars* figures as the licence on the first three films has expired.

Posable, plastic figures by Mego, usually of Marvel heroes or TV characters, are marked in the small of the back. They came boxed or bubbled on card and will be worth much more with the original packaging.

Marx & Co made many plastic figures and clockwork plastic toys in the 1950s and '60s. These included TV characters such as the Flintstones, and Disney spin-offs such as the tiny 'Disneykins'.

Pedigree Sindy Weekender doll,
vinyl, 1963, 12in (30.5cm) high, with box.
£160–180

The **box** increases value considerably. Condition is important, should have no graffiti. If it says 'Made in Hong Kong' on the box should say 'Made in Hong Kong' on the doll (or UK on both) otherwise they do not belong together.

Look at the body – has it **discoloured or melted**? Reduces value considerably.

Solid plastic **body** – made up of parts made in different batches so can have eg browner arms. Does not diminish value. Twist-and-turn waist came later.

Chew marks or scratch marks will reduce value.

Look at **head and hair** – must be in original style, not cut. No missing plugs (no holes) or thinning due to excessive brushing.

Box should have card **neck brace**. Worth more.

Are there missing **fingers**? Reduced value.

Condition of **clothing** is important to value.

Is the **strap** present on box? Worth more.

WHAT HAVE YOU GOT?

Two *Star Wars* figures, R2D2 and C3PO, 1977.
£5–10 each

Palitoy Pippa Princess, 1960s.
£35–40

Palitoy Action Man Eagle Eye Commander, 1978.
£40–45

Mego Marvel Mom and Pop Walton, 1974.
£40–45

Mattel Bubble Cut Barbie Career Girl, c1962.
£250–280

Louis Marx tinplate Disney Dipsey car, 1950s.
£450–500

Teddy Bears and Soft Toys

The best early bears feature sculpted, pronounced muzzles (longer than most modern teddy bears). They have long arms that come below the hip and are wider at the top, then tapered at the wrist with spoon-shaped paws, angling outwards. Their legs are wider at the top, too, with slim ankles and long narrow feet. They also have a slight hump on their backs (like a real bear).

THE BEST teddy bear makers include Steiff, Chad Valley and Schuco. Steiff first made teddy bears in 1902 and from 1904 all their bears had a metal button in their left ear. Chad Valley and Merrythought also used buttons, usually in the right ear, in the 1920s and '30s. A label, or a button in its ear, adds 30–40 per cent to the value.

Rarity also adds value so, as most bears are beige or gold coloured, a black bear will be more valuable. Piccolo bears, made by Schuco in the 1920s and '30s, can be worth a great deal. These come in a variety of colours and some have powder compacts, scent bottles and other novelties inside them. The bear's provenance, or history, will add to its attraction.

Christopher Robin's Pooh bear, bought for him in 1921, was made by Farnell, one of the best English teddy bear maker at the time. Farnell bears remain among the most

collectable of English bears. Others to look out for include Chiltern and Merrythought.

Because of a dearth of mohair during and after WWII, sheepskin bears were produced in England in the late 1940s. These are perishable and not easy to repair. They also have a hard leather backing, making them less desirable than the soft feel of traditional mohair on a cotton backing.

The most collectable bears date from the 1950s or earlier, but Cheeky bears made from 1957 (and still made) have a niche of their own. Post-1970 models are less desirable.

Soft toys are less collected than bears and unless made by

a well-known maker such as Steiff, they are seldom worth much. Quality is an important factor, but its expression and condition are important, too. If a soft toy looks as if it is pre-1950, it could be desirable.

Consult an expert if a soft toy has a silver button in its ear. If you have a quality object, you may do better selling to a specialist or at a specialist sale.

Chiltern, such as this dog on wheels, 1962, is a collectable maker.

Buttons such as **left:** Steiff button or **right:** Chad Valley button can help identify but can be faked.

WHAT TO LOOK FOR...

BEARS

Is it jointed? If the limbs and head move, this is a good sign.

Does it have a sewn nose or a plastic nose? Except for moulded, plastic noses on 1950s Chiltern bears, plastic noses reduce value. Sewn noses, used from 1902 onwards, are preferred.

Does it have glass eyes? First used in 1908, when Steiff introduced them for the English market (over shoe button ones), they are rare in pre-1914 bears.

SOFT TOYS

What kind of animal is it? Monkeys are common and the least valuable. Rabbits, cats and dogs fetch more.

Does it have a tie-in with a book, film or TV show? This can add to interest.

Chiltern Hugmee panda, 1950.
18in (45.5cm) high.
Pandas were second only in
popularity to teddy bears.
£450–500

Cupped ears sewn into
facial seam.

Brown and black **glass eyes**.
These were fixed on with wires
and were sometimes replaced
for safety reasons.

Vertically stitched
shield-shaped **nose**.
Pattern of stitching
can indicate maker.

Velvet **paw pads** have
four claw stitches in
pairs. Pattern of
stitching can help to
identify maker.

Body made of
traditional mohair
on a cotton backing.

WHAT HAVE YOU GOT?

Gabrielle Designs,
Paddington bear,
1970s,
19in (48.5cm) high.
£40–45

Pedigree tiger,
with label,
1950s,
12in (30.5cm) long.
£45–50

Chad Valley dog
with ear button,
1930s,
13in (33cm) high.
£175–195

Merrythought silk
plush Cheeky bear
with label, late
1950s,
14in (35.5cm) high.
£175–195

Schuco pink
powder compact
bear, 1920s–30s.
£400–500

Farnell mohair teddy
bear with boot
button eyes,
1920s.
£1,000–1,500

Games and Puzzles

Edwardian games such as Solitaire, Snakes and Ladders that have wooden boards are sought after, depending on the quality of the board and of the marbles or counters. Chess sets in a good quality wooden box or wooden draughts boards can fetch a considerable amount of money.

CHEAP PAPER and cardboard in the late 19th century combined with the advent of lithographic colour printing, meant that board games with a folding cardboard board (not the canvas used earlier) became widely accessible. Some of the games, such as Ludo and Snakes and Ladders, and their manufacturers, such as Jaques, Spears and Waddingtons, are still around today. Until the 1930s, the playing pieces or figures were often hollow-cast lead by Britains, and these are collectable.

For the collector the ideal is a complete game, with all its pieces, cards, rules and box in good condition. Early examples of Monopoly (introduced in 1935), with its small black box and separate board, are desirable, as is early Cluedo. Risk was first sold in the 1920s and has gone through

many transformations, becoming multi-coloured only after World War II. The dramatic red Risk graphics are well known and sought after.

Cowboy games of the 1950s in good condition might be desirable, as might magic or fortune-telling games of the period. A number of board games with a TV tie-in were produced from the 1960s, such as *The High Chapparal* – a straightforward game with plastic figures which are collected in their own right.

Early wooden jigsaws are collectable, even with some bits missing. You can get a piece specially cut if the puzzle is valuable. There was a craze for puzzles in the 1920s and '30s. Puzzles of the period often come in plain boxes so as not to help the puzzler. These were aimed at an adult market and the more difficult they are, the more they are worth.

Puzzles of the 1950s and '60s are starting to come into their own, but cardboard jigsaws are generally not of much interest. However, puzzles in a series such as the Good Companion puzzles, which are numbered, are collectable.

The price your game will fetch is hard to predict as it will depend on the right buyer being present on the day. The internet is a good marketplace, but make sure you know what you are selling.

Early block puzzles are worth little.

Graphics can be a selling point.

Snakes and Ladders board game, c1910.
With original box and counters.
£20–25

Has all the original **pieces**, dice
and shaker. Important for value.

Has the original **box**, in good
condition. Adds to value.

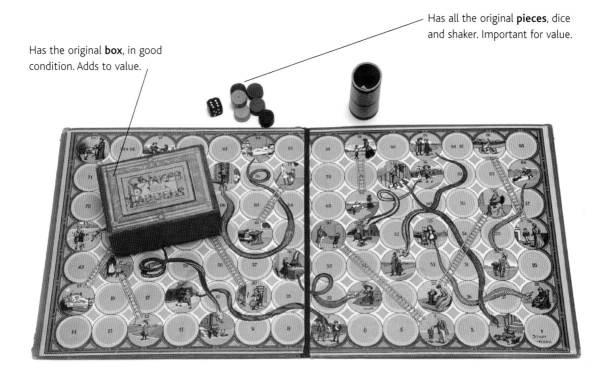

Pre-WWII games came with
separate **box and board**. Need
both to have any value.

Board in good condition and spine
unbroken. Adds to value.

WHAT HAVE YOU GOT?

G. J. Hayter
Victory wooden
jigsaw puzzle,
1950s.
£10–15

Waddington's
Thunderbirds
board game,
1966.
£20–25

Rippon Magic
Blackboard game,
1920s.
£40–45

Wooden Curly
Skittles game,
c1900.
£55–60

Bell Toys &
Games Four
Feather Falls
board game,
1960.
£65–70

Denys Fisher
Dr Who 'War of
the Daleks'
board game,
1975.
£115–125

Silver and Plate

British silver is in the wonderful position of being easy to identify by its hallmarks. These stamped-on marks showng the date, place of assay and maker of the piece are the oldest form of consumer protection, dating from 1544. From that date buyers could confidently expect 925 parts per thousand to be of pure silver.

Between 1697 and 1719 the quality of silver was boosted still higher and Britannia standard introduced at 958 parts per thousand. This standard co-existed with sterling but was rarely used until the early 20th century, when it was the preferred standard for many silversmiths.

Most British silver will be marked on the edge, handle or base depending on the object. The first mark to look for is the lion passant (lion with raised paw), which means the object is silver. Then look for the town mark: London, for example, has a leopard with or without a crown, Birmingham an anchor and Sheffield a crown. Next comes a letter denoting the year it was assayed (marked). Finally comes the maker's mark, often two initials or a pair of two initials. Another mark you may find is a king's or queen's head, which is a duty (tax) mark. There are a number of books are available to look up hallmarks (*see p156*).

Continental silver may be of a different standard. German silver, for example, is marked with an 800 (denoting 800 parts per thousand), a crescent and a star. Fake marks are rare but if you are unsure you can always ask an expert for advice. Silver from the Middle or Far East may not be marked.

Silver plate, copper or nickel coated with a thin layer of silver was introduced to supply a growing market at cheaper prices. At first glance the marks on silver plate can easily be confused with silver marks, but they never include the lion passant. Much plate is utilitarian – knives and forks, dishes and kettles – and was made in huge quantities. It is only worth keeping for sentimental reasons.

The market for silver is variable, with good prices paid for attractive, usable objects in good condition. However, there is little interest in florid designs or pieces that have been poorly repaired. Rarity, quality and condition, all difficult to define, are what makes one cream jug worth more than another. Plate, with the possible exception of designer pieces of the early 20th century, is currently worth very little.

A typical British hallmark will include the lion (silver content), place of assay (here the leopard means London) and maker's intitials.

Plate mark of a similar date. These marks were designed to look like silver marks.

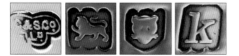

One of a pair of silver sauce boats, by John Pollock, London 1742.
£3,600–4,000

Enamelled scent bottle, by Sampson Mordan & Co, London 1888, with box.
£650–750

One of a pair of silver bowls, by Omar Ramsden, c1930.
£2,700–3,000

Plated table centrepiece with cut-glass dishes, c1860.
£3,500–4,000

One of a pair of Sheffield plated candlesticks, by Matthew Bolton c1810.
£950–1,200

Plated Cube tea and coffee service, by Elkington & Co, c1930.
£1,500–1,850

Silver

Having established that your object is silver, how do you assess its saleability? Look at the thickness of the silver itself. It may have worn away in places with too vigorous polishing, or had some engraving removed, leaving it rather thin. If you run your fingernail gently up the inside of the object you may see a slight 'ripple' on the outside – this will only happen if the silver has become very thin. All repairs diminish value, although well executed, professional ones less so than than crude repairs.

SILVER may have been altered for reasons of fashion or practicality, such as a christening mug turned into a jug. You may be able to tell that the spout of a teapot has been cut-in rather than being 'of a piece'. Forks may have had their prongs replaced, leaving a visible line where new and old metal meet. Ordinary spoons can be turned into apostle spoons, the hallmarks will be correct, but the spoons have still been altered. Joins may be easier to spot when the object is tarnished. All these alterations will diminish value.

Fakes are rare, except in the case of famous and valuable makers. More often an existing object has been 'improved' – for example a Georgian box may have had florid decoration added during the Victorian era, thus reducing its value by 90 per cent. Good, crisp engraving is worth more than if it is worn. Engraved initials or coats-of-arms were often removed after a change of owner, either by polishing off (thus reducing the thickness), or by flooding it with more silver. You may be able to see the outlines of initials if you look carefully in good light – if you can, your object is worth less.

Any dents will deter buyers but they are rarely worth having repaired. All repairs should be carried out by a professional. Do not remove any inscriptions – they may be of interest.

With flatware (knives, spoons and forks) a known maker can significantly increase value. A set of one pattern and maker is more deisrable than a mixed set and plainer patterns sell better. Knives are rare as their steel blades got polished away with abrasive cleaning. Steel blades look dull but are desirable. If the handle and blade come apart, they can be repaired, but leave it to the buyer.

On 20th-century pieces the addition of a retailer's name, such as Liberty or Asprey, will add to value. Buyers, other than serious collectors, often look for practical pieces in pristine condition – an almost impossible combination for which they will pay a premium. Do not overpolish before selling, as this kills the colour and dealers prefer to buy uncleaned items.

WHAT TO LOOK FOR…

Is it properly marked? Check the silver marks in a reference book.

Has it got a retailer's name on it? May increase value.

Is it dented, or in the case of a handle, bent? Any damage will reduce the value, though a small dent can be easily repaired.

Has it been mended? Reduces value.

Has it been altered? Look for a 'seam', which should not be there – for example, to let a spout into a mug to convert it into a jug.

Has a crest or engraving been removed? If the silver is thinner, this may be the case – some of the deeper engraving may show when looked at in the right light, especially if the silver is tarnished.

Has the silver become thin with over polishing? Run your nail gently along the inside of the object – if the silver is very thin, you will see the movement on the outside. This reduces value.

If, for example, a salt or mustard pot, does it have its glass liner? This will increase the value.

Helmet-shaped silver cream jug, made by Samuel Meriton in 1787. In perfect condition this jug would be worth in the region of £700, but as it has been over polished and repaired it is only worth **£70**.

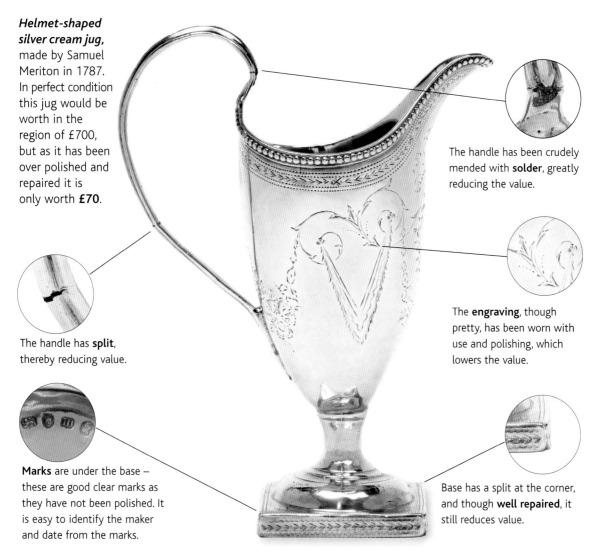

The handle has been crudely mended with **solder**, greatly reducing the value.

The handle has **split**, thereby reducing value.

The **engraving**, though pretty, has been worn with use and polishing, which lowers the value.

Marks are under the base – these are good clear marks as they have not been polished. It is easy to identify the maker and date from the marks.

Base has a split at the corner, and though **well repaired**, it still reduces value.

WHAT HAVE YOU GOT?

Cigarette case, these and match boxes now unpopular. c1931.
£115–125

Bullet teapot by Sebastian Henry Garrard, London 1919.
£150–200

Scent bottle with glass liner, Birmingham 1899.
£220–250

Pair of candlesticks, Chester 1898.
£350–400

Pepperpot in the form of a dog, London 1904.
£400–450

Sugar caster, by Charles and George Asprey, London 1904.
£450–500

Plate

'Old Sheffield Plate' was produced between 1770 and 1840, before it was replaced by electroplate. Old Sheffield Plate was created by placing a layer of silver onto a layer of copper and then rolling it into a single sheet.

AS WELL as being older than electroplate, the quality of the craftsmanship of Old Sheffield Plate is often very high, both of which make it slightly more valuable. It may well be worth keeping rather than selling at the moment. One way of telling if a teapot, for example, is plate, is if there is a visible 'seam', usually to be found along the handle. The seam may be hidden with, say, a beading.

As with silver, much plate is marked with information about the maker. The marks can be found in a number of reference books (*see p156*).

The maker's name can be significant: Elkington & Co is the best name and represents the highest quality. They were able to make items that would not have been affordable in silver, from trolleys for the hotel trade to exotic palm tree table centrepieces. Their name means a higher value. If you can associate your object with a well known retailer, perhaps in a refence book or trade catalogue of the period, it will also enhance its value. The designer's name can be important, for example Christopher Dresser, and the piece may also be numbered and signed. Designs by Dresser were extensively copied, however, so you may need help from an expert in order to make sure your item is genuine.

Styles for plate are similar to those for silver, but because it was aimed at the aspirational Victorian middle classes, styles can be grandiose, but are not fashionable today. Decoration is usually pressed, which may leave it vulnerable to denting.

Plate flatware was supplied in well-made boxes called canteens; these are now extremely desirable (to put silver in) so even if you have lost all the flatware do not throw away the canteen. Sadly, a full plate canteen is worth little.

Plate is rarely faked but sometimes altered, where feet, for example, were knocked off and replaced. Unlike silver, when plate is overpolished the under-metal will show through: yellow in the case of nickel, red if copper. Nickel perishes with age, and any sign of ageing joints will substantially reduce value. Any damage to plate will reveal the under-metal but repairs are expensive and almost never worth it, except possibly in the case of flatware if you want to use it. Take care to go to a reputable source.

Plate is occasionally combined with glass, for example salt cellars and table centres, and can be desirable.

WHAT TO LOOK FOR...

Is it marked? This will increase the value.

Is there a good retailer's name? Asprey, Mappin & Webb and Liberty are retailers that are considered desirable among collectors. Look for their marks inscribed on the underside of the base – these will increase the value.

How stylish is the shape? Very plain utilitarian shapes were often produced in huge numbers and were therefore always very cheap.

Has the silver been polished away to reveal the under-metal? This reduces the value.

How is it decorated? The more stylish the decoration, the more valuable.

Is it damaged? Any denting or damage will substantially reduce the value.

What style is it in? Some styles, such as Art Deco, are fashionable now and therefore more valuable.

Was it made with any glass dishes or liners? If it was, it will sell for more if you have all of the original components.

PLATE 79

Silver-plated entrée dish, c1920.
£15–20

Lids were often swapped. Look for a number on the base and the underside of the lip of the lid. They should tally but when there was a set of three or four matching entrée dishes, they often got mixed up.

Detachable handle. May not be original as does not fit very well. Handles were often swapped by mistake.

Brownish marks are only surface **tarnish** and should polish off with a cloth.

Wear and tear will diminish value.

Plate stamp designed to look like a silver hallmark and with the words 'hard soldered' were intended to convey to the original buyer that this was a good quality object, but does not add value.

WHAT HAVE YOU GOT?

Plated dessert knives and forks with mother-of-pearl handles, in an oak box.
£50–80

Plated cream jug and sugar bowl, 1905.
£80–85

Plated biscuit barrel, 19thC.
£100–120

Sheffield plate entrée dish, c1850.
£300–350

Art Deco Sheffield plate tea service with ivory handles, 1932.
£350–400

Plated cruet set, c1880.
Cruet sets in many forms are currently fashionable.
£400–450

Metalware

Bronze, Brass, Pewter, Spelter and Tin

Over and above the few precious metal objects (gold, silver, platinum) you might find in your home, there are many objects made of non-precious metals, such as fire irons, horse brasses, clock cases or pewter mugs or jugs. Their value lies not in the intrinsic value of the metal they are made of but in their usefulness or their attractiveness.

THE MOST commonly found metal objects are those made of the alloys (mixtures of metals) including brass, bronze, pewter and spelter. The quality of the object may be reflected in the quality of the material it was made of. Thus an ormolu (gilded bronze) clock case will be better quality than one made of cheaper spelter even though the modelling can seem similar. In terms of quality (reflected in the cost of material), the alloys range from bronze at the top, through brass, pewter and spelter to tin at the bottom. In addition these metals can be gilded, patinated (given a surface finish) or painted. Thus painted tin can become tole and, if in good condition, is attractive and collectable, even though when originally made it was cheap and cheerful cottage ware.

Bronze figures were always expensive objects. Look for a maker's name or signature on or under the base. French romantic figures by makers like the Moreau family are very desirable.

You may also find you have objects made of steel, such as fire irons, sometimes polished, which have an attractive light grey finish, but characterized by a lightly pitted surface. This lack of finish reflects the fact that when sold they were seen as purely utilitarian objects not worthy of 'better' metal. Later fire irons, perhaps more decorative in style, are often made of brass. You could also have something made of cast-iron, again a utilitarian metal, such as a door stop or door knocker.

One way of telling all these metals apart is their weight. Cast iron and bronze are very heavy, always solid, whereas spelter or tin are very light in weight and can be hollow. Spelter is often used to counterfeit other more expensive metals by giving it, for example, a gilded finish.

Pewter has touchmarks which equate to silver hallmarks, supervised by a pewterers' guild. The 'recipe' for pewter was changed in 1850 to become Britannia Metal and is marked with BM and the makers' name. It is not generally valuable, though it is collectable if it dates to before 1750. Pewter became popular with Art Nouveau designers for objects such as clock cases which can be desirable.

SHOP WINDOW
Good quality pieces in today's market

Newlyn coffee pot with embossed fish design, c1900.
£120–160

Brass club fender with leather seat, c1900.
£500–700

Bronze figure of a girl, France, c1860.
£300–400

Steel fire irons, c1780.
£450–480

Toleware coal bin with lid, c1900.
£500–800

Cast-iron door knocker, 19thC.
£400–450

Bronze, Brass, Pewter, Spelter and Tin

It is important to establish what metal has been used, as an object made in bronze will be worth more than a similar one made in brass.

Bronze is the ideal metal for crisp casting and was often used for classical statues. The heavier it is the better. It is a yellow metal but is often treated to give it an artificial dark or green surface (patination). When gilded it is known as ormolu and is used for clock cases, furniture mounts and objets d'art.

Brass is the same colour as bronze and can be gilded. It was often used to produce cheaper versions of fashionable or silver shapes such as candlesticks. These are comparatively common and therefore not usually worth very much. Horse brasses are a popular collectors item and have been faked. Look for a blistered or rough cast back, indicating a pre-1920 date. Reproductions have flat, blank backs. Better horse brasses are cast in deeper relief. Royal commemorative ones are very sought after. Brass is also used for fire furniture. Victorian fenders and fire irons are very sought after.

Pewter (a mixture of tin, lead, copper and zinc) was often used for domestic wares such as plates and tankards. It was manufactured in huge quantities and much survives.

Copper is reddish and hard. It was typically used for cookware, such as fish kettles or jelly moulds. The bolder the shape the better. If over polished it can develop small holes which prove its age but diminish its value. It is a good conductor of heat and was used for warming pans and coffee pots. Arts & Crafts Newlyn copper has a distinctive hammered effect rarely seen on other metals. Often marked 'Newlyn' it is very collectable.

Spelter is ideal for casting and was often used to make cheaper versions of fashionable objects and can look very stylish, but is not very durable. Old spelter can look tatty as the finish may wear off after 100 years. It is uneconomic to re-finish it.

Tin was used for basic household items, such as footbaths and cheap flatware, and most has little value. The exception is painted tin, or tole, decorated with floral or landscape scenes. Rarer objects fetch more.

WHAT TO LOOK FOR...

What metal is it made of? May give a clue to the object's quality and value.

When knocked with your knuckle does it produce a sonorous sound? If so it may well be bronze. Often used for good quality objects eg statuettes.

Is it ormolu or spelter? If you scratch it (perhaps on the base or somewhere where it will not show) with a coin and a silvery colour shows through it is made of spelter. Less good quality object, worth less.

If a figure or bust, is it signed? Look on base for script signature. Adds to value.

If made of copper does it have a decorative hammered finish? May be Newlyn and valuable.

Copper jelly mould c1800s.

Tole tray with floral decoration c1800s.

Pewter flagon, c1810,
£100–120

Nice decorative **thumbpiece** – this is a shell but could be a palmette, anthemion or a single or double scroll.

Cover is present – if missing reduces value.

Shape of handle is significant. A simple loop is not as good as a double scroll, as here.

Colour is good and uniform. A nice pale colour without being too clean or too shiny. Adds to value.

Condition is good – very minor wear and tear. Dents will reduce value.

Look for **touchmarks** (like silver hallmarks). May add to value.

WHAT HAVE YOU GOT?

Bronze skillet (saucepan), c1700.
£60–100

Brass tobacco box, with inscription in Dutch, 19thC.
£70–80

Copper footwarmer, c1900. Copper is a good conductor of heat.
£80–90

One of a pair of brass candlesticks, c1830.
£80–90

Art Nouveau oxidised Spelter lamp c1900.
£170–180

Ormolu group of boy and dog, 19thC.
£320–350

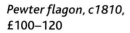

Clocks

Bracket, Carriage, Wall & Mantel, 20th-Century, Watches

Almost every house has a number of clocks dating from different periods. The majority will be late 19th to mid-20th century. This was a time when clocks became more widely available as they were increasingly mass produced, with compromises being made with quality to make them more affordable.

Clocks are unique in that they combine being an object of beauty with a practical household timekeeping device. Their principal purpose is to tell the time accurately, and clocks have therefore often been 'upgraded' to improve their efficiency or just to enable their continued usage, for example the replacement of a wind-up mechanism with an electric one. This considerably affects their value. The quality of the movement will be a defining factor in valuing your clock and also whether it has been altered – you will need an expert to tell you that. A clock with its original movement is generally worth more. The exceptions are decorative French clocks, which are appreciated for their looks, their mechanisms being incidental. George VI replaced many of the movements in French clocks in the Royal Collection with English ones for this reason.

The top end of the clock market has continued to prosper, with the best always finding a ready buyer. This applies as much to a Victorian triple-train, quarter-striking mahogany clock as to a stunning Art Nouveau pewter clock. The slump that has affected brown furniture has to a degree been reflected in ordinary wood-cased clocks with, for example, dark wood longcase clocks becoming less sought after, whilst their country cousins with colourful painted dials are more in demand.

Clocks that are intriguing, such as skeleton clocks, mystery clocks and some early electric clocks, are now much in demand and can command high prices. Rarity is always valued: for example, a miniature carriage clock (less common) will often be worth much more than a standard one, although these too remain very popular.

You might have inherited your grandfather's watch. How do you tell if it is good quality? Look for a good dial, perhaps silvered or enamelled, with gold or silver pinpoint suggesting quality, as do fine blued steel hands. There may be good quality engine turning, engraving or repoussé work on a pocket watch case. If made of gold, silver or platinum a watch will have a value even if only as scrap. All three metals will be hallmarked, giving the date and place of assay. The location may be significant as there are collectors who specialize in particular regional assay offices, such as Edinburgh or Chester.

Liberty Tudric pewter mantel clock, with enamelled dial, c1910.
£4,000–6,000

Porcelain-mounted clock set, France, c1890.
£1,500–2,000

Ever-Ready electric clock, c1902.
£2,000–3,000

Eureka clock, c1906.
£700–850

A bronze-patinated spelter mystery clock, with eight-day movement, France, c1890.
£2,000–2,300

Regency mahogany and brass-inlaid bracket clock, by Richard Webster.
£6,500–7,500

Bracket, Carriage, Wall & Mantel Clocks

How do you tell if you have a valuable clock? You could start by carefully picking it up (never by its carrying handle) and feeling its weight. With the exception of slate clocks, weight is often an indicator of good quality – it was probably expensive in the first place and materials have not been scrimped on.

EARLY CLOCKS have solid oak carcasses veneered in ebony, burr-walnut, mahogany and other exotic woods. Veneering on solid wood is often a sign of quality. Later 19th-century smaller, cheaper replicas of 18th-century originals could be veneered on ply. You might be able to tell by tilting it slightly and looking at the bottom.

18th-century bracket clocks are signed on the dial and the movement in big 'script' letters. The engraving on the backplate is often elaborate and of high quality. They have well-made substantial hands, not, as with later models, hands stamped out of thin metal sheeting. They often have a lever above 12 o'clock to control the strike and are likely to have a fusee movement – like a cone-shaped helter-skelter lying on its side, with a wire or catgut running round it and onto a spring barrel (*see above right*). They were often veneered in a dark wood and have big side glasses displaying the mechanism.

The oldest dials are of cast- or cut-plate brass-mounted with a brass hour ring. Flat silvered dials came in c1775 but are generally 1800 and later. White enamel dials are often French – they were used in the carriage clocks made in France for the English market.

Ormolu decoration, such as figures, often reflect fashionable styles and can be a good guide to dating, but mounts and finials can be an unreliable aid because older styles were revived or old mounts reused. Older cases were also given more fashionable mounts.

The more complicated the movement, the more desirable the clock. Thus one that simply tells the time is less desirable than one that chimes the quarters, strikes the hours and shows the phases of the moon.

In carriage clocks there are degrees of complication in the movement. This, combined with the quality of case decoration, defines its value. Again, weight is often a good sign. Most were made in France, but may have an English retailer's name on the dial. The few English-made carriage clocks have a fusee movement.

A wall clock with a wooden bezel holding the glass is likely to be older and more valuable than one with a brass bezel. Convex glass is older and better, as is an engraved silvered dial rather than white-painted tinplate.

Fusee movement.

WHAT TO LOOK FOR...

Is it solid wood or veneered? Veneered cases often are better quality.

What kind of movement does it have? Ask an expert or research it. It affects value.

Might a wall clock be from a railway station? Sometimes ex-station clocks with the name of a railway are sought after by railway enthusiasts.

If it chimes the quarters, is it twin-train or triple-train? Triple-train is much more valuable. Chimes on bells (like bicycle bells) are more valuable than on gongs (made of coiled or straight wire).

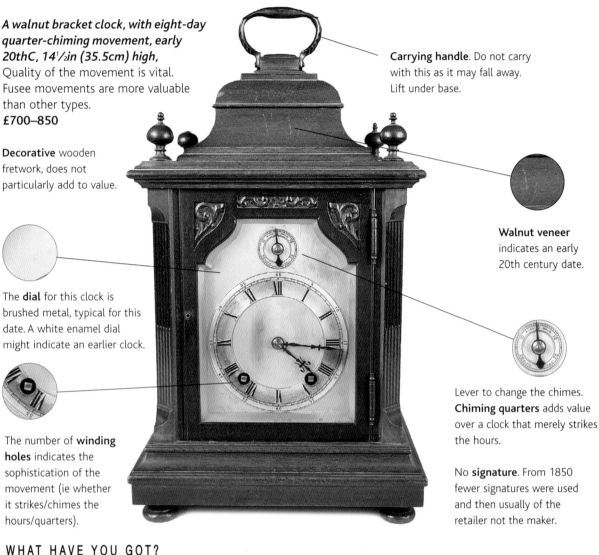

A walnut bracket clock, with eight-day quarter-chiming movement, early 20thC, 14¹/₂in (35.5cm) high,
Quality of the movement is vital. Fusee movements are more valuable than other types.
£700–850

Carrying handle. Do not carry with this as it may fall away. Lift under base.

Decorative wooden fretwork, does not particularly add to value.

Walnut veneer indicates an early 20th century date.

The **dial** for this clock is brushed metal, typical for this date. A white enamel dial might indicate an earlier clock.

The number of **winding holes** indicates the sophistication of the movement (ie whether it strikes/chimes the hours/quarters).

Lever to change the chimes. **Chiming quarters** adds value over a clock that merely strikes the hours.

No **signature**. From 1850 fewer signatures were used and then usually of the retailer not the maker.

WHAT HAVE YOU GOT?

Oak mantel clock, known as a 'Napoleon Hat' clock, 1930s.
£30–40

Slate and cast-brass mantel clock by Vincent & Co, France, 19thC.
£130–150

Carriage timepiece with white enamel dial, with case, early 20thC.
£175–200

Black Forest, carved wood cuckoo clock, Germany, c1875.
£230–250

Gilt spelter clock with porcelain dial and original glass dome, France, 19thC.
£650–750

Mahogany drop-dial wall timepiece, by John Clappison, Hull, c1855.
£1,200–1,400

20th-Century Clocks

At the end of the Victorian era, there was a change of taste away from mainly dark hues to lighter woods and, in the 1920s, the introduction of completely new materials such as Bakelite, plastic and aluminium. The role of the designer became ever greater, with the stress increasingly being placed on the look of the object while the mechanism became standardized and mass produced.

The shapes of 20th-century clocks mirror changes in the rest of the decorative arts. Stylish Art Nouveau mantel clocks in pewter and enamel were superceded in their turn by Art Deco clocks in bright metals and enamels, or in Bakelite. Both are highly collectable. The quality of decoration affects value. Deep,

German wall clock – imported in vast quantities, many are now worn out and generally worth very little.

pastel-coloured translucent enamels used by Cartier in the 1930s for mirrors, compacts and bedside clocks were widely copied. Produced in their thousands, they were cheap to buy and are neither rare nor valuable. For a 20th-century clock to be valuable it usually has to have a big name on it.

Electric clocks originated in the mid-19th century but were not common until the 20th century. Some were driven by mains current, others by batteries. All were made redundant by the quartz timepiece in the early 1970s, which used disposable batteries. Later 20th-century clocks are more about design than about timekeeping.

New types of clock were introduced, including the folding travel alarm clock.

Lalique glass desk clock 'Naiades', c1924. Collected as a piece of art rather than as a clock.

WHAT TO LOOK FOR...

If you have an Art Nouveau or Art Deco clock, does it have with a retailer's or designer's name? The value is enhanced by an upmarket retailer's name, such as Liberty, or designer's name, such as Lalique.

Do you have an early electric clock? Look for the names of the Eureka Clock Co, Synchronome Co and Ever-Ready and for the retailers Harrods and Asprey. These are desirable names. Bulle (French maker of battery clocks) and mains-powered Smith (English) clock are the most common.

Is it in good condition and does it work? Collectors looking for striking design will reject battered or damaged clocks.

*Chrome Starburst clock
by Metamac, 1970s,
23in (58.5cm) wide.
£100–120*

Entirely **new shape**. Breaks way from conventional round and places as much emphasis on the decorative rays as on the face. Interesting to collectors.

Use of **new materials** (chrome) and **new technology** (disposable batteries), adds interest.

Numerals are minimalist, with only 12 and 6 in full, so that the hour marks echo the starburst theme.

Interesting use of **colour** and contrast – red and silver. Will attract collectors.

In good **condition**, no scratches or dents, adds to value.

Shape of the hands very pared down. Typical of the period.

WHAT HAVE YOU GOT?

Enamel clock,
c1920,
4½in (12cm) wide.
£100–180

Silver-mounted
mantel timepiece
by B.J.K. & Co,
Birmingham, 1907,
7¼in (18.5cm) high.
£150–180

Walnut mantel
clock, German,
c1930,
10in (25.5cm) wide.
£150–200

Electric neon
clock, American,
c1940,
10¼in (26cm) diam.
£500–550

Enamel clock,
c1920,
4½in (12cm) wide.
£550–600

Silver-mounted
clock by
Asprey & Co,
1915.
£900–1,000

Watches

If it works, has a good maker's name and is in a precious metal, take your watch to be valued by an expert, such as a watch dealer or specialist auctioneer. If considering selling at auction always ask if they will sell it as an individual lot.

MANY GOLD watch cases have been melted down over the years, leaving behind uncased movements. These can be of interest, as incomplete or broken movements may yield parts useful to restorers. A fusee movement (*see below*) with an intact chain can be worth £35 as the chains are no longer made. A very fine pair of Breguet hands (*see below*) may be worth £10–15, while a lady's polychrome dial (*see below*) is collectable too. Gold dials are often stained and worn but if mint may well be worth something. Movements with

Uncased fusee movement.

Polychrome dial with gold pinpoint.

complications are very much collected: the lack of a case allows you to see the movement. Additional, subsidiary, dials on the front are a clue to complications, as are gongs inside (steel spring-like bands round the edge).

Pocket watches were sometimes converted to wristwatches by soldering on wire lugs, reducing the value. If fitted with a very long strap they were intended to be worn on a pilot's leg in the First World War and are valuable, especially with a provenance.

On a precious metal watch, any engraving will reduce the value, but may add to the value of a non-precious one. They also tend to suffer from wear,

Fine Breguet hands (bottom) are more valuable than thicker ones.

The arrow mark engraved on the back denotes military issue and may add to the value.

WHAT TO LOOK FOR...

Does it work? Gently wind it and if it has not worked for many years a gentle flick in the horizontal plane may set it going.

Is it rubbed? Rubbing on any part of the case will decrease the value.

Do you have an early Swatch in its box? These are also very saleable.

Is it hallmarked? Will have scrap value if nothing else.

particularly the lugs of wristwatches.

Children's watches with automata such as the cartoon character Mickey Mouse or Roy Rogers are very desirable.

If a watch is not working, it is rarely worth restoring before selling. A rare or unusual watch may be, though you will have to weigh up the cost of restoration against a possible sale price. Always get any restoration done professionally; a bad repair can be impossible to undo. Even not working, a good name may well be worth selling.

Rolex bubble-back watch, c1950s.
Signed Rolex, model Oyster Perpetual Chronometer bubble-back, with nickel-plated self-winding movement in a steel two-piece case; screw down Rolex Oyster winder and screwed back, Rolex strap and buckle. This watch was part of the Ravenborg Collection of Rolex Watches.
£1,200–1,500

Look for originality in all parts such as the **winder.**

The original **strap and buckle,** though tatty, may be valued by a collector.

Characteristic **bubble** back designed to accommodate rotor mechanism. Has opening mechanism specific to Rolex.

The rotor mechanism covers the whole **movement**, unlike more modern movements.

WHAT HAVE YOU GOT?

A white metal Mickey Mouse watch, c1950.
£90–100

A mother-of-pearl wristwatch, 1930s.
£135–150

WW1 trench watch, gilt-brass movement, in a steel case.
£150–200

18ct gold open-face pocket chronometer, 1830.
£3,000–4,000

18ct gold half-hunter in case, 1906, 1¼in (3cm) diam.
£1,200–1,500

Cartier 18ct gold tank watch, c1950, 1¼in (3cm) diam
£3,300–4,000

Books

Victorian, Children's and Modern

The majority of books in our houses will be paperbacks that have almost no resale value. Even your hardbacks will need to be sorted into those that may be saleable, including modern fiction and children's books. The internet offers various sites where books can be sold or swapped, so it worth looking at them. A second-hand book dealer might have space for a few books while auction houses are more interested in rare books – especially first editions.

Modern first edition buyers are extremely fussy but if they find a pristine copy they are prepared to pay a great deal for it. The dustjacket may be important, especially if rarely found. It can account for a major part of the value of the book, and loose jackets can fetch high prices in their own right if rare. The jacket's condition may be vital, possibly even more important than the condition of the book itself. Even having the price on the flap can make a difference, as it affects the 'completeness' of the jacket, and also it can be used to determine a first from a later edition. If this is snipped off it reduces the value.

With hardback books remember that condition, possibly including that of the jacket, is all. Rarity will also affect the price. Look at the British Library Catalogue online (www.bl.uk) to see if your book is the earliest edition or a later reprint; they will not always list the publisher but will give the date of first publication. Almost all books will have a date printed on the title page (the page where the book title, author and imprint are set out) and/or on the title verso (back of the title page). If you look at the title verso, you may see a list of subsequent printings, meaning that your edition belongs to the latest of these. First editions are always worth more. With a popular author such as Dickens, there were a number of publishers of his work. You can look on any of the many Dickens websites for a list of first editions. If it is not a first, then an early edition can be good. Later editions, unless a special edition with important illustrations, are worth little.

Illustrations can add to the value of a book, depending on the reputation of the illustrator. Private presses such as the Golden Cockerel Press made a point of using celebrated illustrators and attractive calf bindings.

Leather bindings in their own right generally do not add much to the value of the book unless they are by a known binder, in which case all the value can be in the binding rather than the book. Normally, the collector will be looking for original bindings. Thus a Dickens in its original cloth binding, which was often discarded and rebound in leather for a gentleman's library, is rare and valuable.

Victorian Books

One of the features that you may associate with Victorian books are leather bindings. The different styles of binding – quarter bound, marbled boards, calf or vellum – are generally not as important as whether it is the original binding or a later rebind. A rebinding would be worth less, even if it was a good binding, unless by a well known binder.

ANOTHER BINDING style typical of the period is the so-called '60s (referring to the 1860s) binding. These often complex designs are stamped or embossed onto a cloth binding (*see below*). Many of them are works of art in their own right, which many feel are currently undervalued. Condition is vitally important – if combined with chromolithographic plates, it can add to value.

Good plates add considerably to the value of botanical, agricultural or ornithological titles. Hand-coloured plates are best, but printed plates can be acceptable. Ornithological titles are a popular niche market and books on game birds are sought after. There are many keen collectors in this field so prices are high for books in good condition. Check that all the plates are present, as occasionally plates have been cut out and sold separately as framed prints.

The many Victorian 'how to' books on everything from cookery to manners, often accompanied by small line illustrations, can be amusing, but they are not particularly valuable and you may find a second-hand bookshop is a better bet than an auction house. However, first editions of the most famous of them all, Mrs Beeton's *Household Management*, published in 1860, are rare and therefore valuable. Later editions often have only sentimental value in the family.

Coldstream Guards, 2 vols, 1833. The leather bindings are in good condition but do not necessarily add to the value of a book unless by a well known binder.

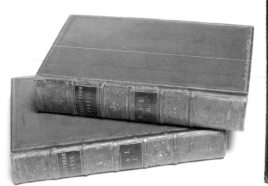

Lewis Caroll, *The Hunting of the Snark*, illustrations by Henry Holdiay. Gilt-decorated red cloth binding.

WHAT TO LOOK FOR...

What date was the book published? Look for a date on the title page.

Is it a first or early edition? More valuable, especially if a first edition.

What condition is it in? Good condition is vital to its value.

Is it complete? If some pages are lost or plates were cut out, this considerably reduces its value.

What sort of binding? Original binding is worth more than a rebound book.

Is a plate hand-coloured or printed? Look for where colour wash, applied by hand, goes slightly over the line, or look for printed dots of colour with a magnifying glass.

Charles Dickens, **David Copperfield, 1850.** The first edition of *David Copperfield* published by Bradbury & Evans.
£450–500

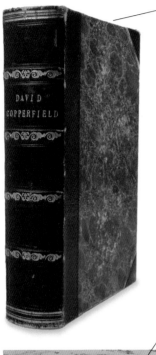

The book form edition of *David Copperfield* was published **bound** in olive green cloth, but it more often appears rebound in half calf or morocco with marbled covers, as here.

All Dickens first editions are **dated** on the title-page. His other publishers include John Macrone, Richard Bentley and Chapman & Hall.

The first edition of *David Copperfield* was illustrated with 40 etched **plates** by Hablot Knight Browne. Other illustrators of his works include George Cruikshank and John Leech.

David Copperfield, like many of Dickens' works, was first published in monthly parts in blue wrappers, in order to keep the public in suspense. They were then published in book form that were often bound up from left-over monthly parts; the **stab holes** where the parts were sewn are sometimes visible at the inner margin (gutter).

WHAT HAVE YOU GOT?

Mrs Beeton's Cookery Book, Ward Lock & Co, 1902.
£45–50

Shakespearean Tales in Verse, McLoughlin Bros, 1880.
£140–160

Conan Doyle, *The Sign of Four,* George Newnes, 1892.
£300–350

Wright's *Fruit Growers Guide,* 6 vols, 43 plates, J. S. Virtue & Co, 1891–94.
£400–450

Kingdon Ward, *Mystic Rivers of Tibet,* Service & Co, 1923.
£460–480

Beverley R. Morris, *British Game Birds and Wildfowl,* 1855.
£600–700

Children's Books

Childrens' books are a specialist market and auctioneers will hold specialist sales on the subject. They need to be in good condition to sell well as, for obvious reasons, they have often been subjected to more wear and tear than an equivalent adult title, so a mint example is particularly rare and valuable.

ILLUSTRATORS can be important: for example, books with illustrations by Rackham and Dulac are sought after. Most modern illustrators do not yet command a premium but attractively illustrated titles such as *Babar the Elephant* or *Orlando the Marmalade Cat* are saleable if in good condition.

Annuals have their own market. Although they have a value, depending on date, they may be lotted up in tens at an auction. It may be worth doing some research yourself.

Try searching the internet for more information on your title. As a good starting point, look at www.abebooks.co.uk (book dealers from all over the world advertise their stock) to get an idea of value. Take care to compare like with like, and do not always assume that the highest prices apply to your annual. It may be that there is a difference in condition, which can make a considerable difference to a book's value, and prices quoted by London dealers will be considerably higher than those achieved at auction.

Beatrix Potter's books have held their value. If in good condition, and it looks similar to the book illustrated on page 97, it may be worth something. Early editions came in glassine covers (a bit like greaseproof paper) and a copy with its glassine cover would be worth much more.

The market in children's books can be volatile, as fashions come and go. It can be affected by a book's connection with a TV programme or film. A good example would be the recent popularity of Tolkein's *Lord of the Rings* trilogy due in part to the success of the three films.

WHAT TO LOOK FOR...

What condition is the book in? Those in good condition will be much more desirable than worn examples.

Is the book illustrated? If so, try to learn about the illustrator. Some well known illustrators' work is collectable in its own right.

If a Beatrix Potter book, does it still have its glassine cover? Most of these covers were immediately thrown away, so a glassine cover increases the value.

Was there a TV series tied in to the book? If so, the book might be more sought after by some collectors.

Is there a niche market for the book? Many collectors will concentrate on a particular area, such as Ladybird books or early editions of *Tintin*. Try searching the internet for current trends.

Stamped cloth bindings are not rare.

Annuals are generally worth little.

The Tale of the Flopsy Bunnies, *written and illustrated by*
Beatrix Potter, 1909.
Frederick Warne became a limited company in 1918, so if the imprint
reads 'Frederick Warne Ltd' this indicates a later printing.
£630–660

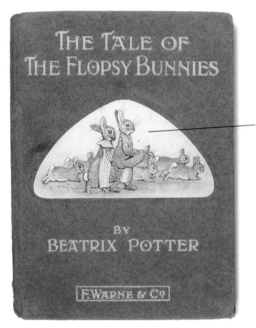

Beatrix Potter's books owed
much of their success to her
own **drawings**, which were
used to illustrate them.

Most of Beatrix Potter's
books first appeared in a
small **format**, bound in
boards with a colour
illustration mounted to the
front cover, as here.

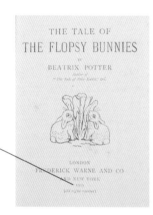

Note the **date** 1909. All but
a few Beatrix Potter first
editions are dated on the
front (not just the back) of
the title page.

WHAT HAVE YOU GOT?

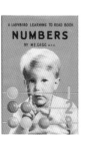

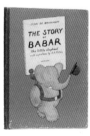

Enid Blyton,
*Five Go to
Mystery Moor*
Hodder &
Stoughton, 1964.
£20–25

Ladybird book:
Numbers,
Ladybird,
1959.
£115–130

Jean de Brunhoff,
The Story of Babar,
Methuen & Co,
1934.
£120–140

*Book of the Flower
Fairies,*
1927.
£160–180

Capt W E Johns,
*Biggles and the
Little Green God,*
Brockhampton
Press, 1969.
£180–200

Richmal
Crompton,
*William The
Lawless,*
Newnes, 1970.
£530–570

Modern Books

The 'Modern First' market is buoyant, with high prices being paid for books in good condition, even for those published relatively recently. Buyers like the book to be as pristine as when it first appeared. These are rare and therefore desirable.

THE JACKET is an important part to a book's desirability. As recently as 40 years ago some book dealers automatically discarded the jacket when a book came into stock. If you have the jacket, it adds to the book's saleabilty. The graphics on a jacket can be interesting in their own right, especially if by a well known designer or artist. Ronald Searle's book covers and illustrations, for example, are sought after.

Look to see if the book is signed or otherwise annotated. It might be of interest, especially if the recipient is connected to the writer in some way (such as his father) or famous in his own right. Collectors prefer a simple signature rather than an inscription to another person. If the author has done a lot of signings, then the rarity value obviously falls. Signatures can also be easily faked.

There are a number of specialist collectors of, for example, cookery books. This has been a huge growth area and there are specialist sales to cater for it. Generally, it is pre-1850s cookery books that are valuable. Of particular interest are books annotated by the author or books used by them to research a project, such as recently came up in a sale of books from Elizabeth David's library. If you have a miscellaneous collection of 20th-century cookbooks, these are best sold to a local book dealer, as the value would be too low for an auction house. Check out the prices on abebooks.co.uk to get an idea of value – the lower end of a range of values will be more realistic.

Travel books are also sought after by collectors of Modern Firsts, but much of collectable travel writing is antiquarian.

WHAT TO LOOK FOR...

Is the book in good condition? This is extremely important to collectors – even a slight stain to the page edge can cause a drop in value.

Is the jacket in good condition? Any damage will reduce value, including the price being clipped off.

Does it fit a genre? If there is a niche market for it – for example cookery – it may do well in a specialist sale.

Is it a first edition? Check the date on the title page and the title verso for any reprints listed. Look here also on more modern titles for a sequence of random numbers – if it contains a 1, the book is a first edition. This can make a big difference to its value.

Is it a hardback? Paperbacks are rarely considered valuable as most books are published first in hardback.

Cookery classics can be valuable.

Travel books are a new collecting area.

Ian Fleming, Goldfinger, *published by Jonathan Cape, 1959.*
The first edition was published by Jonathan Cape, as were nearly all of Ian Fleming's works.
£80–120

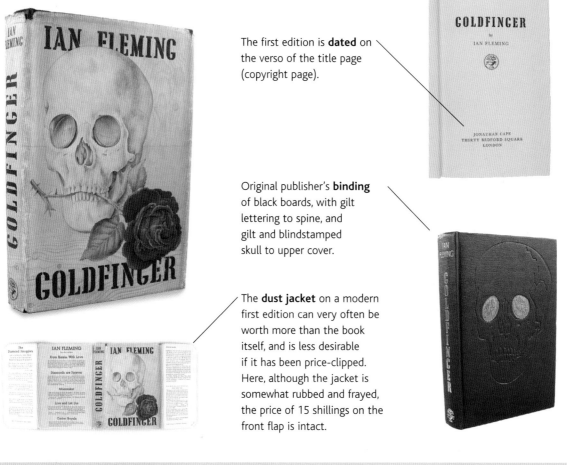

The first edition is **dated** on the verso of the title page (copyright page).

Original publisher's **binding** of black boards, with gilt lettering to spine, and gilt and blindstamped skull to upper cover.

The **dust jacket** on a modern first edition can very often be worth more than the book itself, and is less desirable if it has been price-clipped. Here, although the jacket is somewhat rubbed and frayed, the price of 15 shillings on the front flap is intact.

WHAT HAVE YOU GOT?

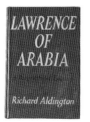

Richard Aldington, *Lawrence of Arabia,* 1955.
£45–50

P. G. Wodehouse *Quick Service,* first edition, Herbert Jenkins, 1940.
£155–175

Sylvia Plath, *Aeriel,* Faber & Faber, 1965.
£220–250

Agatha Christie, *At Bertram's Hotel,* Collins Crime Club, 1965.
£300–335

George Orwell, *1984,* Secker & Warburg, 1949.
£340–360

Patrick O'Brien, *Master & Commander,* Collins, 1976.
£400–440

Jewellery

Victorian, Paste and Costume, 20th-century

Almost all the jewellery found at home will have been made in the last 150 years. Before 1850, fine jewellery was the preserve of the aristocratic elite and is now rare and expensive. In the 1850s, new gold deposits increased the supply and allowed the introduction of new, lower, 9, 12 and 15 carat standards. This, combined with new, innovative, mass production techniques based on stamping, rolling and pressing, created new affordable jewellery, but not always of high quality.

EVEN THOUGH some of the finest diamond jewellery was produced in the late 19th century, traditional Victorian star brooches, crescents and sprays are not currently in fashion, but if a piece is pretty, well made and wearable it will find a market. Enamelled decoration, if in good condition, is desirable.

Following WWI, a new pared-down 'Modern' style established itself with a more angular, geometric Art Deco look, often with diamonds set in platinum instead of gold. If you could not afford the real thing, authentically designed copies were sold in a wide range of new and innovative materials: Bakelite, plastic and synthetic gems. Many of these are collected today.

The stark 'utility' post-WWII years, when luxuries were highly taxed, were a period of stagnation in jewellery design but were the prelude to the jewellery revolution in the 1960s. Big and bold was in, with textured surfaces and abstract designs highlighted by uncut gemstones and crystal groups not considered 'suitable' for jewellery until then. The designer became more important. Signed pieces by designers of this period such as Andrew Grima and John Donald are highly collectable. Much modern jewellery is of commercial quality, probably of cast and assembled construction and, if gold, is probably machine made. It has little resale attraction, and may have only scrap value.

Two pairs of late 18th-century chandelier earrings. **Left:** diamond set: look for a harder, sharper and more brilliant look. **Right:** paste set: similar setting but the 'stones' will have a 'deader' look but because they are old they are still valuable.

SHOP WINDOW
Good quality pieces in today's market

Victorian diamond star brooch.
£800–1,000

Paste clip brooch with fitted case by Jourado, 1930s.
£200–250

Cultured pearl necklace with sapphire clasp, most of value is in clasp.
£200–250

Silver and mother-of-pearl cufflinks, studs and links, 1930s.
£250–300

Bird brooch with ruby eye by Cartier, c1940.
£2,400–2,800

Platinum, sapphire and diamond ring, c1920.
£2,500–3,000

Victorian/Fine Jewellery

If you have inherited some jewellery, what do you look for? The best pieces will be well made and solid. Feel the weight of the piece – heft it in your hand. If it feels good, it probably is good; but if it feels light and flimsy it is probably not worth much. Condition is vital to price, so dents or missing parts will considerably decrease the value.

VICTORIAN jewellery is often gem set, the most important pieces with rubies and sapphires. The stones' quality varies enormously, but often the brighter and more vivid the colour of the stone, the more valuable. Rubies are often small, so beware of larger red stones. Semi-precious stones such as amethysts (mauve) and citrines (yellow) are common, often used for the lower end of the market, and less valuable.

Animal brooches, such as lizards, owls and frogs, some realistically modelled and set with diamonds, are desirable. However, small lightweight bar brooches are of little interest.

Gem-set rings with good stones are valuable but less good quality dress rings, unless 12 or 15 carat gold, are not worth much. Many are worn, as are signet rings, and this affects the value. Wedding rings of the period, likely to be 22 carat, only have scrap value.

Sentimental jewellery, such as mourning rings or brooches often in jet, onyx or black enamel, or the Mizpah brooch (given to a loved one going overseas), may be of interest but are not valuable.

If silver, heavier weight or pretty pieces such as lockets, chains and anything with enamel work will be saleable.

Jet was much loved by the Victorians but the 'real thing' is difficult to identify.

From left to right: natural pearls, cultured and imitation.

Ring settings – claws should be undamaged.

Look for hallmarks inside the band.

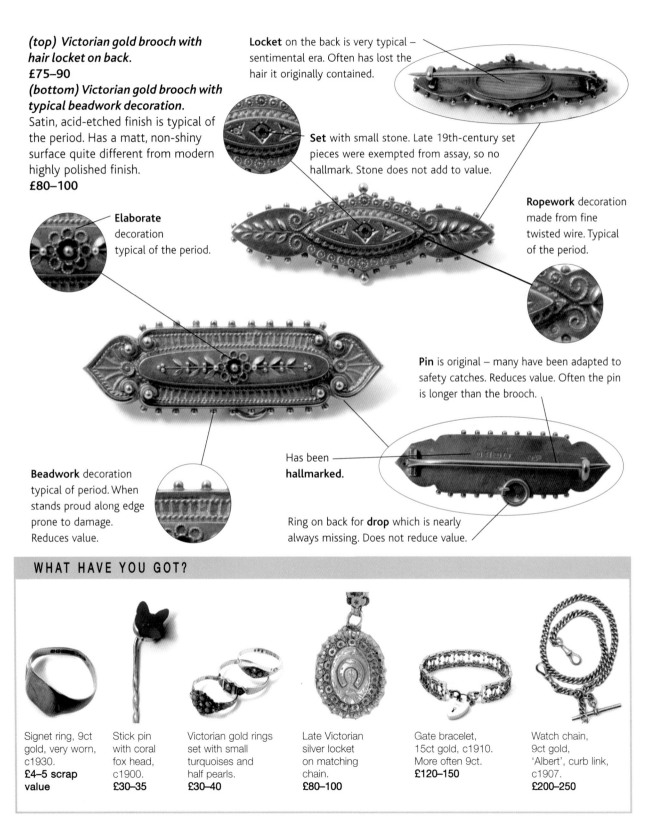

(top) Victorian gold brooch with hair locket on back.
£75–90
(bottom) Victorian gold brooch with typical beadwork decoration.
Satin, acid-etched finish is typical of the period. Has a matt, non-shiny surface quite different from modern highly polished finish.
£80–100

Locket on the back is very typical – sentimental era. Often has lost the hair it originally contained.

Set with small stone. Late 19th-century set pieces were exempted from assay, so no hallmark. Stone does not add to value.

Ropework decoration made from fine twisted wire. Typical of the period.

Elaborate decoration typical of the period.

Pin is original – many have been adapted to safety catches. Reduces value. Often the pin is longer than the brooch.

Beadwork decoration typical of period. When stands proud along edge prone to damage. Reduces value.

Has been **hallmarked.**

Ring on back for **drop** which is nearly always missing. Does not reduce value.

WHAT HAVE YOU GOT?

Signet ring, 9ct gold, very worn, c1930.
£4–5 scrap value

Stick pin with coral fox head, c1900.
£30–35

Victorian gold rings set with small turquoises and half pearls.
£30–40

Late Victorian silver locket on matching chain.
£80–100

Gate bracelet, 15ct gold, c1910. More often 9ct.
£120–150

Watch chain, 9ct gold, 'Albert', curb link, c1907.
£200–250

Paste and Costume Jewellery

There are arguments over who 'invented' costume jewellery, with Coco Chanel's colourful imitation jewellery of the 1910s usually credited with being the first. Paste, using glass instead of precious stones, had been made since the 18th century but the majority is either Victorian, Edwardian or post-1920.

OFTEN INTENDED to replicate much more expensive pieces, old paste can be stylish and desirable. If set in a white metal it may be silver so look for hallmarks, although if made abroad it will be un-marked. Old paste often mimicked diamonds, but some has coloured foil behind the glass, or makes use of other coloured 'stones'. Paste of the 1940s and '50s is a whole new ball game: designers such as Schiaparelli used new colours and shapes for chunky bracelets and earrings. These are much sought after if signed.

Coloured glass beads. Could date from the 1920s through to the 1950s. Fun but not valuable.

Bakelite jewellery first became popular in the 1930s. It came in a huge range of colours and could be cast or carved. It was used for bangles, bead necklaces, buttons and brooches, which are highly collectable today. It is comparatively rare and valuable.

Some of the best post-war costume jewellery is signed. If it looks and feels substantial and stylish it will be have a value.

Plastic was widely used for expensive, designer jewellery in the 1960s. Parisian couturiers, such as Lanvin, explored a new range of jewellery shapes, creating space age pendants combining plastic and chrome. The high-quality Vendome range used plastic and crystal to create striking strings of beads. Plastic was also used for cheap 'fun' jewellery. Often larger than life, it is characterized by bright colours and is highly collectable.

Large plastic flower earrings, 1960s: are collectable but not expensive.

Gold coloured metal jewellery is worthless unless designer made. Look at the back to see if it is signed.

WHAT TO LOOK FOR...

If paste, are all the 'stones' present? If any are missing, it will reduce the value.

If paste, what colour is it? Imitation diamonds may be Edwardian but more intense colours and irregular shapes may indicate 1950s paste. Both are collectable.

How heavy is it? If light, it may be base metal. Smell it – base metal has a metallic smell. Not worth much unless signed.

Is it signed? A 'good' retailer or manufacturer's name on the back such as Trifari or Corocraft will add to value.

Is it Bakelite or plastic? If Bakelite, it will date from the 1930s and be worth more than 1960s plastic.

Is it in good condition? Condition is vital to value.

Paste 'ruby and diamond' necklace in original box, c1820.
Replicates the style of an authentic ruby and diamond necklace. Missing drop or pendant.
£700–1,000

Original box always a good sign. It is a good quality box the therefore object inside it was probably expensive when sold. Adds to value.

Use of **coloured 'stones'** adds to interest.

Set in silver – **hallmarked** on clasp.

Missing drop or pendant. Would marginally add to value if present.

High quality setting – a more valuable piece.

WHAT HAVE YOU GOT?

Silver and amethyst brooch, c1920.
Small brooches not fashionable.
£5–10

Brass and glass mouse brooch, 1950.
Animal brooches are collected.
£15–20

Pair of plastic and metal earrings, 1960s.
Sixties jewellery is collectable.
£20–25

Bakelite bangle, 1930s.
Rare and therefore collectable.
£60–70

Gold-plated flower bracelet and earrings, 1940s.
£60–70

Art Deco silver pendant necklace, set with paste stones, 1930s.
£100–115

20th-century/Modern jewellery

Art Nouveau shapes lent themselves to jewellery, with twining naturalistic forms. On the Continent, designers such as Lalique pioneered the use of *plique-à-jour* enamel, while in England Liberty-style jewellery was produced by designers such as Archibald Knox, Charles Horner and Jessie King. It was affordable and stylish, usually made of silver, often combined with iridescent enamelling or set with semi-precious stones.

JEWELLERY after the Edwardian period is characterized by a move away from gold to lighter coloured metals. At the high end platinum became fashionable and was often combined with diamonds to create the characteristic cool, geometric Art Deco look: clip and double-clip brooches (*see below*), panel brooches and bracelets. Look out for 'calibre' cut coloured stones (usually rubies and sapphires) used as a contrasting design feature, which makes a piece especially desirable. The quality is supremely good and the jewellery highly saleable.

Only the elite businesses – Cartier, Van Cleef & Arpels, Boucheron – signed their jewellery. Fake signatures do exist and the most expensive jewellery was copied in paste, distinguishable by its duller 'stones' and lighter weight.

Jewellery of the 1940s and '50s is often referred to as 'Retro' and its collectability is variable. Large brooches featuring yellow gold in bright polished finishes, sometimes in conjunction with rose and/or white gold and partly gem set, are not fetching high prices and perhaps should be kept until fashions change.

'Modern' jewellery of the 1960s is often bold and abstract. Designers such as Ken Lane 'borrowed' ideas from ancient Greek and Indian jewellery as well as 1930s Cartier. His glamourous pieces, such as

Diamond and platinum double clip brooch, c1920, front and back view. The back is often a good indicator of quality with sophisticated fittings.

Deco earrings typical of the period. Paste versions were made so weigh to see if they are platinum and look at the quality of the fittings.

knuckle-duster rings, huge earrings and jewelled collars, were worn by Jackie Onassis. and Elizabeth Taylor. These are widely collected.

In the 1970s gold was cheap and chunky gold chains, up to 30in (45cm) in length, often with a large pendant set with an inexpensive stone such as rhodochrosite, opal mosaics or lapis lazuli. These have a value, if only for their weight.

Plique-à-jour *enamel brooch,*
14ct gold set with pearls and a
pearl drop, American, c1900.
Classic Art Nouveau shape. Very
desirable. Naturalistic forms
adorned with pearls, from nature.
£600–700

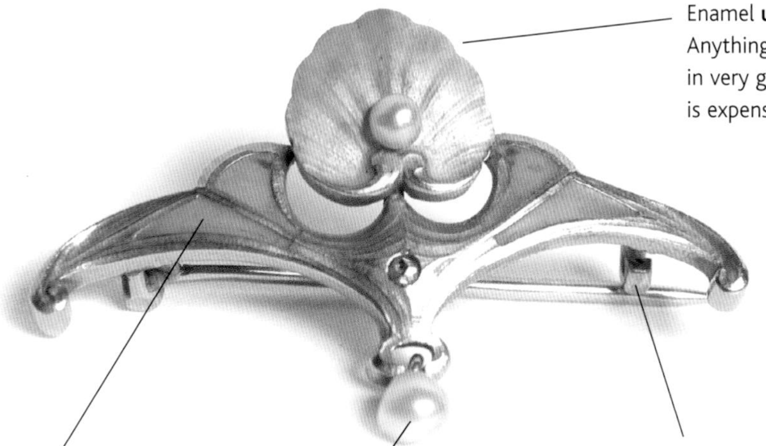

Enamel **undamaged**.
Anything enamelled must be
in very good condition as it
is expensive to 'mend'.

Plique-à-jour **enamel** –
has no back (like stained
glass). Very typical of
period. Pink less common
than blue or green.

Original pin and catch.
Often replaced later with
safety catch. Reduces value.

Original **pearl drop** present.
Often they have been lost.
Adds to value.

WHAT HAVE YOU GOT?

Ken Lane
enamel ring, 1960s.
Price dependent
on condition.
£70–100

Silver and
diamond watch,
1930s.
Diamond weight
determines value.
£100–250

Art Nouveau 9ct gold
brooch,
by Murle Bennett, set with
a turquoise cabouchon,
c1925.
£500–550

Wendy Ramshaw
gold, pearl and
peridot pendant,
1970s.
£600–800

Amonite, peridot
and gold pendant,
by Andrew Grima,
1972.
£900–1,000

Diamond and
platinum pearl
drop earrings,
c1925.
£1,000–1,200

Fashion

Clothing and Accessories

When faced with a cupboard full of old clothes it is tempting to reach for the nearest bin liner and take them all to the charity shop. That might be a mistake as many clothes and accessories are now collectable – 1960s sunglasses or rayon scarves just as much as 1950s party dresses.

IN VINTAGE FASHION, one of the most important considerations is condition. However, with much historic fashion – for example, a Georgian flower-embroidered waistcoat – rarity will be what gives it its value. Many buyers will want to wear what they are purchasing, so holes, snags, armpit stains, weak shoulders or broken zips are a complete turn-off. Add to this the fact that buyers like a complete item, not just shoes in pairs, but all three pieces (jacket, trousers and waistcoat) of a three-piece suit. Many serious collectors of vintage clothes will only buy items that have their original label, unless you can supply proof of age, such as a dated photograph from a family album. Unless labelled, do not expect to net a fortune.

Keep your market in mind when trying to sell – think about where your garment would sell best. Your local auction house may not be interested in fashion. A truly vintage item, such as a 1920s beaded dress or Victorian embroidered bag, would perhaps do best sold at a specialist auction – many of the large auction houses hold regular Street Fashion and Vintage Fashion auctions. There are also traditional dealer's shops. The easiest way to find someone local to you is to search the internet for 'vintage fashion'. You may also get some idea of prices, though remember that dealers' prices will almost certainly be higher than what you would get for your item. Alternatively, you could sell through an internet auction house such as eBay or via your own internet website. If you do, be clear about your descriptions, especially sizing and condition, and photograph as many details as possible.

No one will want to buy your items if they look or smell used or dirty. Serious vintage sellers will always clean clothes before selling them. However, many older clothes will not have a care label giving washing instructions (unusual before the 1970s), and you will have to decide how best to clean them – or if to risk it at all as you never know the outcome. The rigours of the modern washing machine, even on the 'gentle' wool cycle, will be too much for garments intended to be carefully hand-washed. For some articles it might be best to take advice from an expert dry cleaner who is used to handling delicate items. For leather shoes and handbags a gentle rub with a duster or some neutral colour shoe polish can get rid of the dust and bring out the life in the leather.

SHOP WINDOW
Good quality pieces in today's market

Beaded chiffon evening dress, decorated with glass beads, 1920s.
£580–650

Hermès crocodile-skin bag, 10in (25.5cm) wide, 1960s.
£1,300–1,500

Take Six man's floral satin jacket, c1960.
£220–250

Bective Chiquita shoes with diamante decoration, 1950s.
£145–160

R. W. Forsyth silk top hat, c1900.
£120–140

Vintage Levi 501s.
£300–350

Clothing

To identify what you have got, hang clothes up against a door and look at the cut, style, length and fabric. Try to identify what period they belong to: a mini skirt, for example, could be 1960s, while a long flowery Laura Ashley skirt probably belongs to the 1970s, and A-line skirts were popular in the 1950s.

THE FABRIC can help you confirm a date. Most of the fabrics used for Victorian and Edwardian clothes were natural (wool, cotton, silk), but from the 1920s synthetics and from 1938 nylon were used. The thread used in the stitching and the type of finish – hand or machine – are also clues, as are the type of fastenings, for example buttons, zip or Velcro. The zip brand and its position are good indicators of period: side seam zips below the armpit were used from the 1930s to the '60s. From the 1970s centre back zips were almost exclusively used.

A couture Dior dress will be made from top quality fabric, have a fine seam finish with bound edges, careful pattern matching, a quality zip and buttons and, hopefully, its original label. A more humble dress from the 1960s by, say, Richard Shops, will use less expensive fabric, have seamed joins where the fabric print may not match, and the overall level of finish will be lower.

Finally, flick through any family photographs to see if you can find any of the clothes being worn. Collectors will find added interest.

Vintage styles are currently available in the high street but some buyers prefer the original. Retro post-war fashion is popular, especially 1950s day dresses and authentic 1920s beaded dresses. Oriental-style fashion, be it Lagerfeld prints or a kimono, is also popular.

Victorian Paisley shawls or christening robes are sought after mostly for use. The size of a christening robe is critical as babies today are often larger when christened.

Christening robe, white cotton lawn with lace trim, Victorian.

Top: Utility clothing label.
Below: Horrockses

Zips are an important indicator of age and quality.

WHAT TO LOOK FOR...

Is it worn out, torn or stained? If the answer is yes, reserve it for a car boot sale or charity shop – it will not be of interest to collectors unless it is rare.

If it is synthetic, then what is it? Acetate, nylon and lycra all have specific introduction dates, so your garment cannot pre-date this benchmark.

Is there a label on a vintage fashion item? These are usually reliable. If you can see one, this is a fabulous signpost that will help you decide on an attribution. Designer, manufacturer and care labels can be significant to buyers and thus add to the value.

Rose print cotton day dress, 1950s.
It has no label. Not too serious as it
has all the other quality features.
50s style is a very distinctive look
and is very saleable.
£75–85

The **cotton is crisp**. Sign of quality.
No fading or wear. Adds to value.

It has a **YKK zip** from Japan.
Again shows quality, more
expensive. A cheaper dress
or one made at home would
have a cheaper zip.

The even **pleating** at the base of
the bodice is more complex than
simple gathering. A sign of quality
and therefore worth more.

The rose **print** is very detailed
and finely printed in the new
stay-fast inks. A sign of quality.

Machine stitched (not home-sewn
from pattern). Puts it in a different
category. More valuable.

WHAT HAVE YOU GOT?

Marks & Spencer
stretch nylon and
lycra swimsuit,
1960s.
£30–35

Laura Ashley
printed cotton
maxi skirt,
1970s.
£40–45

Acetate summer
dress with
Cort zip,
1960s.
£45–50

Howe Street
Hawaiian shirt,
1950s.
£55–60

Frank Usher floral
print Tricel cocktail
dress with
Lightning zip,
1960s.
£75–85

Charles Butter
Utility suit,
1940s.
£115–130

Accessories

Shoes, hats, bags and sunglasses mirrored the fashions that were set by clothes. They may also have a historic link; for example, the wedge shoes of the 1970s were a revival of those of the 1940s, which in turn looked back to the wedges of the 1920s.

SHOES may be datable by style. Look for where they were made: a possible clue is the sizing (an English 6 or Continental 39); vintage shoes have the width, too – a printed stamp in black or gold under the tongue or on the strap. Look inside the shoe for the maker's name. The original shoe box will add to value.

Utility footwear went hand in hand with Utility clothing and had the same Utility label (*see page 110*) and is desirable. Shoes sold by shops like Dolcis in the 1940s and '50s were good quality shoes. Shoes by classic makers such as Rayne are one step up, but Biba shoes or boots are at the top of the league.

Until the 1930s all hats were hand-stitched and finished. The lining was the last thing to go in, so anything sewn through the lining is a later addition and

reduces value. A 1930s hat may have a loop of wire to secure the hat to the head; in the 1950s a V-shaped wire clamp was used. If a hat is crushed or out of shape, it will not sell.

Bags are big-time! If it is American it will almost certainly sell well. Condition is a vital factor. If you have a clutch bag with rhinestones, a few have probably fallen out. Leave any repairs to the buyer as a bad repair diminishes the value. Lucite (clear Perspex) bags were popular in the 1950s and today top quality bags are very desirable. The 1960s was a period of *faux* leather and plastic. Vinyl can wear, so check for cracks. Brand names such as Gucci and Hermès were huge in the 1950s, '60s and '70s.

Scarves and ties are going through a revival, with retro chic dictating that both skinny and 'A' line kipper ties can be worn. They are probably best sold over the internet.

Retro sunglasses are popular. The lenses are not as protective as modern ones but can be replaced. Sunglasses must be in pristine condition, with the plastic shiny, not dull and sweaty. Polaroids from the 1960s are the height of fashion.

WHAT TO LOOK FOR...

Are shoes and gloves real pairs? It is easy to confuse two similar shoes.

With shoes, what material are they made of? It varies with fashion. Snakeskin was popular in the 1920s, while crocodile and lizard were used during WWII as they were not rationed.

With a bag, is it marked? You may need a magnifying glass to see minute makers' marks on the clasp or even the frame. It may seem to have no mark, so look closely. A mark adds to value.

Is there a mark on the frame of a pair of sunglasses? Frames are usually marked, which helps to identify the brand and attracts a buyer.

Crocodile-skin handbag c1950.

Snakeskin shoes, 1930s.

Union Jack handbag, 1960s, 11in (28cm) high.
Evokes the strongly nationalistic feeling that swept British style in the 1960s. 'Wow' factor is high – it is a statement bag with broad appeal. It goes with '60s Pop culture, signifying a moment in fashion and reflecting the new affluence of the young. Would not have been expensive when bought, probably from a department store.
£50–60

Made of **vinyl**, used in a very clever way. More interesting to buyer.

Has 'Made in Britain' **zip**.

Condition is good. Not much damage, so must have been little used. Adds to value.

Good **size**. Not too big so does not put people off.

No **maker's name**. Not significant here as it is iconic.

The **edges** are clean and unfrayed. Adds to value.

Good **colour** combination. Striking not dreary. Will sell better.

WHAT HAVE YOU GOT?

Tootal printed rayon scarf, 1960s.
£20–25

A *faux* straw and net hat, 1950s.
£55–65

A pair of leather and suede shoes, made and retailed by P. Beeson, Paris, 1940s.
£75–85

A pair of Astro-Matic plastic sunglasses, with original box, 1950.
£90–100

Beaded evening bag with brass clasp, Victorian, 7in (18cm) high.
£145–165

A silk and wool Paisley shawl, 36 x 64in (91.5 x 162.5cm), 1870–80.
£400–450

Coins and Medals

Coins, Medals

Great artists and designers produced coins and medals, creating miniature works of art. The quality of their workmanship is what makes them desirable. Prize or commemorative medals are also collectable, and many are on specialist subjects such as ballooning or medicine, adding to their collectability.

THE COIN WORLD has two sorts of collector; the general collector who loves the idea of owning a piece of history, and the specialist who only wants exceptional examples and whose interest is kindled by a coin's artistic or academic merit. That is where the big money is. An example can be seen in the sovereign shown on page 117: generally sovereigns are worth merely their bullion value – about £80 – but because this example is of greater age and in mint condition it is worth a little more.

If you find a mixed bag of old coins in your attic, they are unlikely to be worth much, but you should always check before disposing of them. Go to a dealer or specialist auctioneer who may spot an interesting item that a general auctioneer may not. Valuable coins in your family will probably always have been treasured and most likely kept safe in a box or cabinet. If so, they have often developed a surface patina (sheen), which is much valued by collectors. Do not on any account touch or pick them up with your fingers. A single fingerprint can ruin the patina built up over decades. Handle as little as possible, if at all, and only by the edge. Never clean or polish a coin.

Most medals that have been kept in the family will have been handed down with a story attached: Great-uncle George fought at Gallipoli, was wounded in the leg and always walked with a limp. It may not seem significant to you, but part of the allure of medals to a collector is the history that comes with them. Real people fighting through world changing events, and the medals are a tangible record. So if you are thinking of selling some medals, it is important their story goes with them, and any correspondence or photographs you might have, especially of Great-uncle George wearing the medals or in uniform, will make a medal more interesting to a collector.

WWI and II medals were issued in considerable quantities and are, therefore, relatively commonplace. The most valuable are those whose history sets them apart, such as those awarded to women or those associated with a particular event. One example is the group on page 119 belonging to the Naval Commander who took the decision to scuttle the crippled HMS Edinburgh, rather than risk the rest of the convoy, despite the fact that she was laden with 40 million pounds' worth of Russian gold destined for America.

Coins

Originally coins were worth their weight in gold, or silver, or whatever metal they were made of, which is why the copper cartwheel 2d (*see page 115*) had to be so big – it contained 2oz of copper. Today, many old coins are still only worth their bullion weight. It takes a rare and special coin to be worth much more.

AGE DOES not necessarily mean value. Roman coins may be worth little, particularly base metal examples.

Early English coins, such as a medieval example, will have the king's portrait on one side and the moneyer's name and the mint on the other. A rare mint is worth much more. From the 14th century, coins can be dated by the mint mark. Later coins may have the designer's initials incorporated into the design. Local and national museums have coin collections to visit; the Fitzwilliam Museum and the British Museum both have information online, and if you think you know what you have got, research it on the internet, but beware – the internet can be misleading. There are many reference books available, many of them very academic but also accessible ones such as

the price guides published by Spink (for example *Roman Coins & Their Values* and *Coins of England*).

Until the mid-17th century, silver coins were often 'clipped' – part of the edge was trimmed off so that the clippings could be sold. The first coins with a milled edge (tiny ridges) to discourage clipping were issued during the reign of Elizabeth I and they became standard from 1662.

When there was a shortage of small change, banks and retailers issued tokens. In the 18th-century, examples were for the first time also produced specifically as collectors' items, and many of these are today highly collectable.

Coins have been faked since antiquity. Usually only an expert can distinguish a fake, although some modern copies are fairly obvious.

WHAT TO LOOK FOR...

Is there no date on an English coin? Dates did not appear on English coins until the mid-16th century. If you cannot find a date, this will indicate that you have an earlier coin.

Is there a mint mark? Some mint marks are rare and will increase the coin's value.

Is the coin clipped? Some are severely clipped and this much reduces their value.

Is there a milled edge with tiny ridges? The coin was probably made from 1662 onwards.

What condition is the coin in? Dents, scratches and wear are a minus when selling, as are coins that have been mounted as jewellery – the mount often damages the edge or, even worse, some coins have a hole drilled for a chain.

Silver denarius of Hadrian (AD117-138).

Silver penny of William the Conqueror (1066–87).

Victoria copper penny, 1853

The value of a coin is dependent on condition. This penny is in mint condition.

£400–500

Obverse

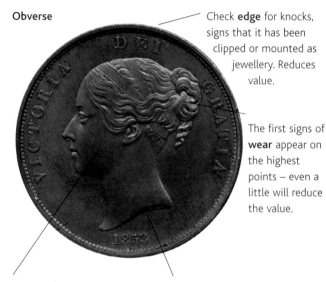

Check **edge** for knocks, signs that it has been clipped or mounted as jewellery. Reduces value.

The first signs of **wear** appear on the highest points – even a little will reduce the value.

On British coins it is a tradition that the **bust** of each monarch faces in the opposite direction to their immediate predecessor.

This is called the **truncation.**

Reverse

Some coins have milled edges or edge **inscriptions** – originally intended to prevent clipping. The Latin inscription on the current £1 coin, DECUS ET TUTAMEN, means 'an ornament and a safeguard'.

Space known as the **exergue.** This is often where the date is found.

Britannia first appeared on Roman coins, but the first representation on British coins is in 1672, on a farthing of Charles II.

WHAT HAVE YOU GOT?

Bronze AE 3 of Valentinian I AD 364–75.
£3–5

Copper token, Kelly's Saddlery, Strand, London, 18thC.
£50–60

Royal Horticultural Society silver prize medal, 1864.
£80–100

Queen Victoria gold Sovereign, 1887.
£100–120

George III copper cartwheel twopence, 1797.
£120–150

George V silver crown, 1933.
£160–200

Coins not shown actual size.

Medals

One of the most common medal groups is 'Pip, Squeak and Wilfred' (after a cartoon in the Daily Mirror), the three campaign medals of World War I: the bronze star, silver war medal and brass victory medal.

THE FIRST MEDAL to be awarded to all ranks was the Waterloo Medal in 1816. The General Service Medal was introduced by the navy and then the army for those who had fought in the Napoleonic Wars, but it was issued only to survivors in 1848, making it rare and valuable. Many have a number of campaign clasps – the more clasps the more interesting and valuable.

The many colonial wars and campaigns of Queen Victoria's reign each had their own medal. Boer War medals can have up to 10 bars (campaigns), adding to their value. Crimean War medals, especially relating to the Charge of the Light Brigade, are desirable. They were not engraved with the recipient's name.

Six and a half million WWI groups were awarded, so they are common. The group was sent to the family of those killed with a memorial plaque (*see below*); if this is included with the medal group it is worth at least twice as much. If the memorial plaque is for a woman, it is worth even more.

Most medals awarded during WWII were not impressed with the recipient's name, making it difficult to identify the owner, unless the group includes a Military Medal or Territorial Army medal, which were engraved or impressed with the recipient's name. A typical group might include the Victory medal, given to everybody, a 1939–45 Star, awarded to those in an operational area for six months, and a campaign medal for Italy or the Far East. Other medals were awarded for bravery such as the MC (Military Cross). The George Cross and Medal were awarded to the police and wardens for acts of bravery during the Blitz. German medals are also sought after.

WHAT TO LOOK FOR...

Does the medal bear the cameo portrait of a king or queen? This can help to identify it. The reverse usually identifies the campaign.

Does it have a bar or bars on the ribbon with names of places or campaigns? This will add to its interest.

Does a medal from Queen Victoria's reign still have the box it was posted in? Increases value.

Does the ribbon have a small oak leaf on it? The soldier was mentioned in dispatches; adds to interest.

Is the ribbon faded and worn? Many Victorian medals were worn on a daily basis and are therefore show wear. New ribbon for most medals is available today and can be replaced for display purposes. Do not dispose of the old ribbon.

WW1 death plaque.

Polar medals are rare and valuable

Group of medals of Vice Admiral Salter who, as Commander of HMS Foresight made the decision to scuttle HMS Edinburgh in 1942 despite the fact she was laden with Russian gold.
£21,000–23,000

Ribbons may be **worn** and tatty but this is part of the medal's history.

The **colours** of the ribbons can help to identify a campaign, eg the Egypt medal is blue and white symbolizing the River Nile.

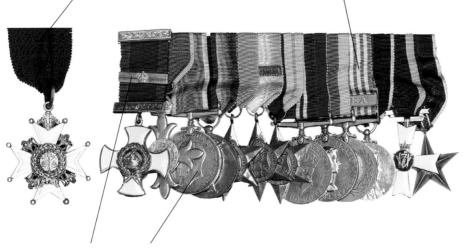

Does the ribbon have a **clasp or bar** with a place or campaign name on it? Adds to interest and therefore value.

The **head of the monarch** will help to identify and date a medal.

Look on the **reverse** of the medal to see if it is inscribed with the recipient's name. WWII medals are not incribed, though medals for gallantry, such as the Military Cross are, and can help to identify the group. Adds to value.

WHAT HAVE YOU GOT?

German Iron Cross, with ribbon, 2nd class, 1939.
£55–65

WWI group of Private H. Gayton, RAMC.
£75–100

General Service Medal 1962.
£90–100

WWII group and OBE of Colonel Thomas Lindsay.
£320–420

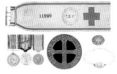

WWI nursing yeomanry group with Red Cross armband.
£450–550

Victoria Crimea medal, of Rifleman J. Pine
£470–500

Ephemera

Photographs, Cigarette cards, Postcards

Collectors of ephemera are an idiosyncratic bunch, since the things that appeal to them are often the things that most of us have thrown away over the years such as old postcards, stamps and programmes. The value is in the eye of the collector.

COLLECTORS can be divided into those who want to display their items and the more academic who keep them in albums. In either case, rarity and condition are what they are looking for. When selling ephemera it is vitally important that you talk to a specialist dealer or auctioneer. In general, a local auction house will not recognize or be able to authenticate, for example, an autograph, and will therefore undervalue it.

Autographs are a minefield – even for an expert – as so many were faked. Expert knowledge of who did or did not sign their letters or who sent out well-crafted (and so hard to distinguish) printed or autopenned versions is vital to establishing a value. You need expert knowledge to distinguish the good from the ordinary; for example, a 1948 cricket bat autographed by the Australian team (the Invincibles) might be worth £150 but was, in fact, worth £1,000. So it is worth doing your homework before deciding on where would be the best place to sell.

You can find useful information on the internet, but you have to be sure you are comparing like with like. Spend time asking and, hopefully, finding answers to questions – what does an authentic Marilyn Monroe autograph look like? With repeat items such as theatre programmes, which may appear for sale a number of times, it is easy to establish a value. However, with unique items, such as a letter, it is much more difficult, and you also have the thorny problem of authentication. It is therefore best to ask an expert for advice.

For most auction houses the minimum value of a lot in this field is £35, so if you have items such as postcards that are worth less, it may well be worth selling them over the internet. There is an international band of collectors out there waiting for a golden opportunity, so ensure that you have correctly identified and valued what you are selling.

With stamps, too, a considerable degree of specialist knowledge is needed to be able to identify stamps of different dates and printings. It is very small differences that significantly affect the value. There are, of course, reference books and if you have a number of stamps, or an album, it might be worth consulting one to try and identify those that you think might be of interest to a dealer. Any that are damaged, or cut down, unless rare, will not be of any interest.

Photographs, Posters and Programmes

Home photos are not of much interest to collectors unless they feature unusual or interesting people, places or events. Of more interest are albums of life or work abroad before WWII. Advertising posters were usually stuck to walls and destroyed, so they are comparatively rare and can be valuable.

PRESS OR PUBLICITY photographs are more collectable than home photos. Better quality production, both in the thickness of the paper and the processing, make them more desirable. Press photos may have a stamp on the back, a date or a note of the day it appeared. Dating evidence like this can help. Publication annotations, such as the name and date of publication, even a typed and stuck-on byline or description add to the value.

Signed photographs of 'stars' may be of interest, depending on the personality and number of photos they sent out: one of Judy Garland would always find a buyer. Photos by well known photographers such as Cecil Beaton, Norman Parkinson or David Bailey are also sought after.

Titanic publicity brochure, c1912. Anything relating to the *Titanic* will have a value.

Photo albums that may have belonged to grandparents or great-grandparents depicting their life and work while, for example, in the colonial service in India, are collectable if in good condition. The story that goes with the album adds to the value, especially if you can identify the places and people.

The older an advertising poster the better. If in good condition, with good quality artwork and interesting graphics or subject, they are desirable. Some printers' work is more collected than others; look for the printer's name at the bottom – it does not always appear, but good quality ones often do.

Fans of a particular star or football team are keen to collect memorabilia, including programmes. Sporting

Posters in good condition are collectable.

WHAT TO LOOK FOR...

Do you have a photo album of foreign travel photographs? If pre-WWII, it may be of interest.

If you have a poster, is it badly creased? Crease marks are accepted but if the paper along the creases is worn away it reduces the value.

Do you have ephemera that would appeal to a specialist group? If it will appeal to a niche market, such as theatre fans, may be saleable.

Do you have any old football programmes? These may be of interest to fans, especially if linked to a memorable game such as the the FA Cup Final. Certain teams such as Manchester United and Chelsea are more collectable than others.

collectables, particularly football and golf ephemera, is a strong market. Price is dependent upon age and rarity.

Theatre programmes are not as collectable, but the same criteria apply. A show that ran for ages will have supplied many programmes, but there may be lots of potential collectors who saw it. Obscure productions in far-flung places are less likely to find a buyer unless they feature a budding star.

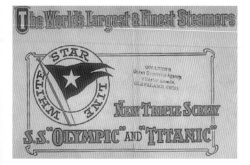

Programme for The Mikado *by Gilbert and Sullivan, performed at the Savoy Theatre, London, 1885, 9 x 5 ½ in (23 x 14 cm).*
The comic two-act opera was performed first here and ran for 672 performances.
£25–30

In good **condition**.
Adds to value.

Interesting period **graphics**.
Makes it more collectable.

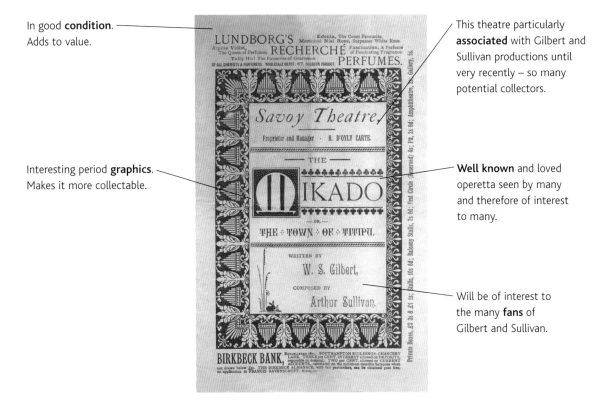

This theatre particularly **associated** with Gilbert and Sullivan productions until very recently – so many potential collectors.

Well known and loved operetta seen by many and therefore of interest to many.

Will be of interest to the many **fans** of Gilbert and Sullivan.

WHAT HAVE YOU GOT?

FA cup final programme Chelsea v Tottenham Hotspur, 1967.
£5–10

London Palladium Programme, starring Judy Garland, 1951.
£15–22

Ovaltine, advertising poster, 1950.
£55–60

Promotional still/press photo for publicity, – Marlene Dietrich, 1950–60.
£145–165

Cinema poster, *A Day to Remember*, 1953.
£155–175

Felice Beato Nautsch Dancers, India, albumen print, 1858.
£300–350

Cigarette cards, Labels and Trade cards

Cigarette cards were first produced in Britain in reasonable numbers in the 1890s, but the 'golden age' was from the 1900s to 1930s. Age is important in establishing how much they are worth but it is not everything.

BIG MANUFACTURERS such as Wills and Players produced imaginative series of cards on subjects such as sports or movie stars. There were also informative and educational series. Many cigarette cards were re issued, so look on the back – an authorized reprint will say so. Rare card reprints are still sought after. If framed up it can be hard to tell which is a reprint. There are also fakes, which you may be able to spot as they often look new and the printing is rather flat.

Many companies produced a pre-printed 'lick and stick' album for their cards, and most cards were collected in this way. An empty album is rare and can

be worth more than a filled one. Similarly, loose cards are generally worth more. So do not put loose cards in an album.

Trade cards were often used in shops to promote a brand. They often ring a nostalgic bell with collectors. Cards associated with popular films such as *Star Wars* have a greater value than their age warrants. The Brooke Bond Tea cards (*see below*), like cigarette cards but in packets of tea, can be seen advertised on the trade card.

Labels are a new collecting area with buyers interested in subjects such as wine, cheese, or beer labels. Labels may be regarded as miniature works of

Labels are a new collecting area.

art, often by good designers, and with attractive and innovative graphics. Condition and rarity are the bywords.

WHAT TO LOOK FOR...

What condition is a cigarette card in? Collectors ideally expect them to be in pristine condition and they will fetch a great deal more if they are.

Is a cigarette card an original or reprint? If it was an authorised reprint it will say so on the back. Rare cards reprinted for nostalgic reasons are less valuable than the original but still sought after.

Do you have an empty cigarette card album? These are rare and can be worth more than one with cards in.

Do you have a collection of beer, wine or cheese labels? If in good condition they may be collectable, especially if rare.

Star Wars cards are collectable.

Trade card for Brooke Bond tea cards.

Wills cigarette cards of radio celebrities in their purpose-printed album, 1934.
Millions of these were printed and collected so most are not rare, and therefore not valuable.
£4–8

Pre-printed **album**. Empty albums are rare and can be valuable.

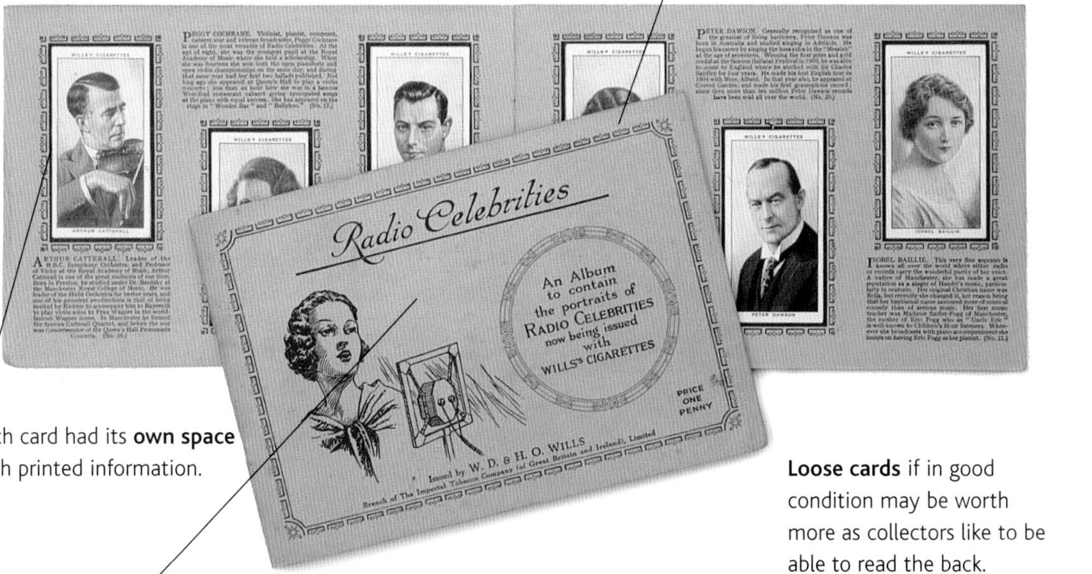

Each card had its **own space** with printed information.

Loose cards if in good condition may be worth more as collectors like to be able to read the back.

In good **condition**. As so many were printed it must be pristine to have any value.

WHAT HAVE YOU GOT?

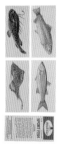

Carreras,
Sport Fish,
set of 50,
1978.
£1–5

Taddy & Co
Clowns & Circus
Artistes, reprint,
1939.
£5–10

Brooke Bond
tea cards.
(see trade card
opposite).
£5–10

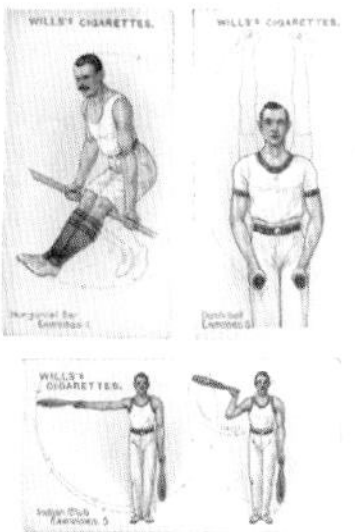

Wills Physical
Culture,
set of 50,
1914.
£35–40

Players
Footballers'
Caricatures by RIP,
set of 50, 1926.
£50–60

Gallagher signed
portraits of
famous stars,
set of 48, 1935.
£95–110

Letters, Postcards and Stamps

Letters and autographs can be a minefield. The signatures of the famous have been replicated since 1897, when Queen Victoria's thank-you letters after the Diamond Jubilee were all printed. Stamps are less collected than they were, but rare examples can be very valuable.

LETTERS PURPORTING to be from famous stars were often done by secretaries in a cinema studio. John F. Kennedy had three secretaries trained to write like him so all his correspondence appeared to be answered personally. The Beatles' roadies did a good line in autographs.

Letters are a slightly safer bet as it is not generally worth forging a two-page letter if it is only worth £50. If genuine and by someone famous, or infamous, it will have a market. Show it to a specialist auctioneer or dealer and get an opinion.

Postcards were produced in their millions for holiday-makers to send home. Most popular were those of well-known beauty spots and tourist destinations, and the saucy seaside postcards. These are seldom worth much. It is the good photographic cards of small villages or of now-lost country pastimes that are desirable. Another collectable area are postcards with advertisements by firms such as Cadbury's or one of the tobacco companies, as the designers they used were the best of their day.

At the top end of the market are the Art Cards produced by artists such as Mucha and Toulouse Lautrec. Mucha was a top designer and worked for Sarah Bernhardt.

Stamps have fallen from favour. There are fewer collectors and they are fussier. Rarity and quality are the most important factors, followed by condition. If stamps are torn or frayed or have cut edges they will be of little value. Anomalies increase the value, such as when Mauritius printed 'Post Office' instead of 'Post Paid' on one of its stamps in 1847. The higher the face value, the more valuable it is likely to be as fewer will have been sold or used. Modern first editions are worth little.

Royal or commemorative postcards can be collectable.

Letter written by Paul McCartney, damaged, but still collectable, c1964.

A collection of Cape of Good Hope, triangulars from a penny to a shilling.
Earlier stamps are crudely printed and were cut out of a sheet. Perforations came in c1850s.
£600–800

Look for a **watermark** in the paper. These have an anchor watermark.

If **paper** has a bluish tinge may be an earlier printing and worth more.

Bears trace of Cape of Good Hope **postmark**. May interest collectors.

Has a BONC (barred oval numeral cancelar) **postmark**. Can be of interest to collectors.

Stamps that have been **cut out** are of an early date. If you have stamps with perforated edges that have been trimmed down, this greatly reduces value.

WHAT HAVE YOU GOT?

Mabel Lucie Atwell postcard, very popular so not rare or valuable.
50p–£1

Postcard of keddle net fishing near Rye, 1905, 5in (12.5cm) wide.
£15–20

Scrap album with numerous postcards, paper cuttings and drawings, late Victorian
£25–45

Letter from Richmal Crompton with a corrected proof of *Wiseman's Folly*, 1958.
£55–65

Framed letter from Queen Victoria, 8¾ x 7in (22 x 18cm), 1857.
£100–120

£1 black Postal Union Congress stamp, 1929.
£300–400

Modern Technology
Household Appliances and Cameras

The history of the 20th century can be read in its household appliances. The developments in science and technology that brought electricity, plastic and radio waves was expressed in the home in toasters, telephones and television sets. As with many other collectable areas, the role of the designer became increasingly important, and it is this that interests many of the modern technology collectors as many of the designs are ground breaking.

IN THE 1960s and '70s designers like Dieter Rams at Braun were redesigning and redefining what the new generation of advanced electrical goods would look like. Some household objects have become iconic, such as the Kenwood Chef, which represented both a technical advance and a revolutionary design concept. This was the first of its kind and, like the Mini, set a design precedent that has evolved into the modern food processor. The rapid development of new technologies, in the second half of the 20th century particularly, both in terms of materials and capacities, presented an opportunity for designers to express their ideas in objects such as radios, typewriters and home stereos. Many of these have become highly collectable.

With electrical goods, always test before using or selling. Fifty-year-old wiring may prove to be a hazard, especially if the appliance has been kept in a shed or attic. It should be checked out by an expert. Old equipment can be converted using modern cables, but this must be carried out by a qualified electrician. Most collectors of telephones will be more interested in them if they work. Indeed, working period electrical goods can have a lucrative rental market in the world of TV drama.

Cameras, by contrast, with a few notable exceptions, are not usually collected for reasons of style. Their aficionados are more interested in the technical specification, with the most money going to those with the highest specification in any particular range. The basic post-war Rolleiflex Automat is worth only £30–40, whereas the top of the range Rolleiflex is worth £800, and special editions even more.

The digital revolution has had a marked effect on the camera market, with famous names such as Nikon, Canon and Olympus film cameras falling considerably in value despite their technical sophistication and brilliant picture-taking capabilities. Even the antique wood and brass cameras of the late 19th and early 20th centuries have fallen in value. Collectors have gone cold having seen the value of their collections fall, leaving the market over-supplied with mainstream brands. Only the rare and distinctive will now fetch a good price.

SHOP WINDOW
Good quality pieces in today's market

Ecko AD65 round Bakelite radio, 1933.
£500–550

Cream Bakelite telephone, 1930s.
£220–250

Sinclair Neoteric stereo amplifier, 1968.
£100–200

An Edwardian hand-operated 'bellows' vacuum cleaner, c1905.
£100–150

Wood and brass Lancaster quarter plate camera, c1895.
£200–230

Rolleiflex twin lens reflex camera.
£800–850

Household Appliances

Interest in gadgets and appliances has more to do with style than with technology. The collector can afford to be fussy, millions of most household appliances were made, and they can afford to wait for one in perfect condition. A tatty vacuum cleaner will not be of interest unless it is a particularly rare model.

Hacker Herald radio, 1960s.
Such radios are very collectable.

COLLECTORS are usually interested in specific types of objects, so someone interested in Art Deco Bakelite telephones will not want to know about tape recorders. With telephones, unusual colours such as green or red, rather than the usual black, will increase the value. Collectors of telephones generally want them to work. Talk to a dealer about how to go about it.

Radios are collectable: 1920s ones by Art Deco enthusiasts, as well as those made in the 1960s. The best known brand is Roberts, but those by Hacker (*see above right*) are on a par for quality and can be even more collectable. Those with VHF are more valuable than those simply with long wave and medium wave.

Ground-breaking designs of the 1960s and '70s are particularly sought after. A good example is the Olivetti Valentino typewriter designed by Ettore Sotsass as an 'anti-machine machine'. It abandoned its bulky cast-iron predecessors in favour of light, modern, colourful plastic. Similarly, Dieter Rams, chief designer at Braun, re-thought record players, separating the speakers to cater for stereo sound and creating a compact unit in the greyish-white colours that typified such electrical products for two decades.

So how do you know if something is a design classic? Reference books will help but also do some searching on the internet. It is important, too, to find the right place to sell. There are specialist dealers, and some auction houses hold specialist sales.

WHAT TO LOOK FOR...

Is it stylish? Collectors look for eye-catching, classic design.

Is it in good condition? There are many of these objects around so collectors can afford to be fussy and wait for the rarer ones in good condition. Flaws are acceptable in only particularly rare models.

Is it clean and dust free? It must be well presented for collectors to be interested.

Is it safe? Get all electrical items checked before selling. Electrical wiring can be updated, but make sure you use a qualified electrician.

What colour(s) is it? Good colours will always be of interest to collectors. Some colours are very representative of their eras, such as orange and the 1960s.

Reel-to-reel tape recorder, 1960s.

Sinclair Micromatic miniature radio, 1967.

The first Kenwood Chef, 1950s.
Stylish eye-catching design – has become a design classic. 'Good' design always of interest to collectors, so will add to value.
£100–150

In **working order**. Adds to value. Collectors may not want to use it but they would like it to work. Always get electrical appliances checked for safety.

All **accessories** in place. Adds to value. Bowl is glass and has often been broken, lost or chipped.

Use of **coloured plastic** attractive to collectors.

Minor wear but no major dents, cracks or damage. Adds to value.

WHAT HAVE YOU GOT?

Singer sewing machine, made right through 20th century.
£10–15

Bakelite Supreme hairdryer, rarely found in good condition, 1940s.
£15–20

Hoover vacuum cleaner, 1950s.
£20–40

A Calor aluminium, electric toaster, 1930s, 8in (20.5cm) wide.
£40–45

JVC Video-sphere Space Helmet TV, 1960s.
£100–300

Braun music centre, 1956.
£1,000–1,200

Cameras

Classic wood and brass cameras in good condition are still sought after by collectors and fetch good prices. They are seldom faked but are still occasionally made. At the opposite end of the spectrum is the box camera, found at most car boot sales, which sells for a few pounds.

SOME KODAK cameras are more valuable than others. The Beau Brownie decorated with an Art Deco front panel or with a souvenir front panel, such as for the World Fair, are very valuable. This is a good example of cross-collecting since such a camera would be of interest to Art Deco enthusiasts, as well as to camera collectors.

Unusual colour variations are desirable. For example, the blue and green miniature Bakelite Coronet cameras made in the mid-1930s are sought after as much by collectors of Bakelite as camera buffs. Coloured cameras, rather than the conventional black or silver, were often produced to appeal to a 'ladies' market. These are rarer since fewer were sold and now command a premium. Look out for other unusual variations, such as folding cameras with red, rather than the usual black, bellows. These are worth more.

Cameras with multi-speed shutters and high-quality lenses always fetch more in any particular range. The number of shutter speeds marked on the ring round the front of the lens will tell you if it is multispeed. The lens may be labelled, for example anastigmat which, with some research, is a good indicator of quality. A low f.stop, such as 3.5, indicates a better lens than a higher number; 6.3 or 7.7 are more common, and allow less light through the lens, and are therefore less good. SLR (single lens reflex) lenses may go down to f1.4 or less and are collectable.

Many cameras are sold over the internet. Seller beware:

ensure that you know what you are selling. There are so many models available, even within a single make or date, some rarer and more valuable than others, and it takes an expert to know which is which. Take it to an expert for advice.

The majority of cameras are not valuable. However, they are undervalued at the moment so rather than sell perhaps you should start your own collection.

Leica IIIf with case, lens & instructions.

Zeiss Ikon 1950 Super Ikonta.

Zeiss Ikon Contaflex Super Synchro, c1960.
Classic mechanical single lens reflex (SLR) camera.
£60–70

Meter window on front of prism housing indicates has coupled exposure meter

Usually comes in an ever-ready (front hinges down) case. **Case** not of much interest. Collectors will display uncased.

Shutter speeds marked on the lens an indicator of quality.

Body is in good condition. Shows few signs of use – always worth more.

Has a good quality **four-element Tessar lens**. Reliable but not top of the range.

WHAT HAVE YOU GOT?

Kodak Brownie basic box camera,1930s.
£5–10

Kodak 1A metal and leather folding camera, c1914.
£5–10

Kodak Retinette IIB compact 35mm camera, with case, 1958–59, 5in (12.5cm) wide.
£25–40

Yashica Atoran sub-miniature 9.5mm camera, c1965, 4½in (11cm) wide.
£30–35

Zeiss Ikon Maximar A207/3 plate camera, 1927–39, with leather case.
£90–100

Sporting Antiques

Equipment and Memorabilia

Sporting antiques are popular at the moment, often fetching good prices. Sporting antiques may be divided into equipment and memorabilia, though most are bought to display rather than use. The exceptions, such as croquet sets, some golf clubs and fishing reels, should be in serviceable condition as the potential buyer will want to use them.

Sporting memorabilia, be it ceramic, silver or glass, is in the fortunate position of having two potential buyers: one is the collector of, say, Staffordshire bowls (*see page 136*), and the other is the cricket enthusiast who wants to buy it for the scenes painted on the side. The quality of the object itself is paramount, so look, as you would on any ceramic object, for marks or signatures to indicate the manufacturer.

With a metal object, work out what it is made of. A figure or model made of spelter will be worth less than a bronze one, and much less than a silver one. In the case of silver, look for hallmarks to get a date and place of assay, as a silver object will be worth more than a similar one made of silver plate. Check too that it is complete, including, for example, glass liners, spoons or lids. If silver or plate objects are dented, it reduces their value, but it is unlikely to be worth repairing them before selling.

Sporting equipment can be tricky to evaluate as it may come in a number of ranges, some of them better quality. Thus the 'Wimbledon' fishtail tennis racquet (*see page 137*) is a desirable 'brand' and worth considerably more than one with not such a good name. To fetch a good price, early gutta-percha golf balls should have the characteristic mesh pattern and be hand-hammered (and therefore irregular), not the mechanically produced versions pressed in a mould. There are also rubber practice balls with the same surface pattern but which do not have much value. Equipment intended for use, not display, should not be woodwormed after being lost at the back of the garage for 20 years, or bent from having been shoved into a box. Condition is important to value. Reels should spin evenly and not get stuck – they will if the rim is dented from having been dropped.

When considering selling, check internet auction sites to give you some idea of value. However, selling over the internet is both time consuming and often disappointing. If your object is in good condition, you may do better selling direct to a dealer. Go to an antiques fair and look at dealers' stock to get an idea of prices. If you have a large quantity of items to sell, consider taking a stall at a fair yourself. There are also specialist sporting auctions, although smaller items may get missed if they are lotted up with a number of other objects.

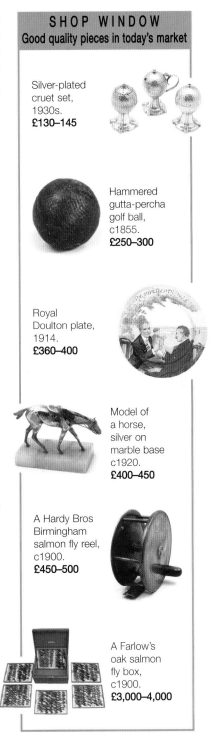

SHOP WINDOW
Good quality pieces in today's market

Silver-plated cruet set, 1930s.
£130–145

Hammered gutta-percha golf ball, c1855.
£250–300

Royal Doulton plate, 1914.
£360–400

Model of a horse, silver on marble base c1920.
£400–450

A Hardy Bros Birmingham salmon fly reel, c1900.
£450–500

A Farlow's oak salmon fly box, c1900.
£3,000–4,000

Equipment and Memorabilia

Leather items, such as cartridge bags, fly wallets or golf bags should be in good condition. Leather responds well to a clean with furniture wax or leather cream. Cartridge bags are often bought to be used; the bigger the better. The bladder inside an old leather football can be replaced, but this is best left to the buyer.

CLOTHING worn by top personalities, such as football strips, jockeys' silks or cricket blazers, as well as antique football boots or boxing boots, is sought after. Sporting caps, often velvet, may have a value, depending on quality and condition. International caps are worth much more.

The value of wooden items, such as bats and racquets, is dependent on quality and condition. The Bradman bat and the 'Wimbledon' tennis racquet (*see page 136*) are particularly valuable because of the brand name and associations. Without the names they would be worth much less. Items signed by a well known sportsman or team are considerably more valuable.

Tennis racquets are popular collectors items but the price depends on whether it has, for example, the original stringing as well as on the quality of the brand and maker. Sets of wooden bowls are collectable, too, and may come in a case. If they are made of lignum vitae, a beautiful wood, they are collected both for display and private use. The case is not important unless it is of good quality leather which adds to the value.

Paper items, such as a flicker book (*below*), need to be in good condition to be saleable. Buyers will want to be able to read or use it without it falling apart. Books on sporting subjects are sought after, particularly shooting and fishing.

Is it in good condition? If it is dented, or has parts missing or falling apart, it will be valueless.

Is it complete? Something like a croquet set should have all the pieces, but missing hoops can sometimes be replaced.

Does it work? A fly reel, for example, is well engineered and should spin smoothly. However, if it has been dropped and the rim dented, it will stick.

Is it signed? Bats and balls can be signed by individuals or teams. If they are famous or are of local significance, it may add to value.

If a bag or case, does it have all its straps and buckles? Adds to value if it does.

An early Staffordshire cricket bowl, c1870.

H. W. Austin, *'Flicker' No. 9, Forehand and Backhand Drives*, published by Slazengers Ltd, London, c1920.

A fine quality croquet set, made by F. H. Ayres, c1920.
The 'Wimbledon', with four boxwood head, ash handle mallets, six hoops, four coloured wooden balls, pegs, a wooden mallet and other accessories. The set is in its original pine box with the paper trade label for F. H. Ayres. Although Wimbledon is commonly associated with tennis, it was also the home of the All England Croquet Club, founded in 1868.

£200–400

Hoops: there should be six. If one is missing it can be replaced it is expensive.

Box in **good condition** with original label – adds to value.

Mallets should be **heavy and solid.** Inferior woods are much lighter.

Mallet shaft may be split. Reduces value as expensive to replace.

Mallet heads should ideally be boxwood. If split devalues set.

Balls should be nice and round. If wood they may be chipped or dented. They should all be of the same pattern. Balls may be composite; does not reduce the value.

WHAT HAVE YOU GOT?

A pair of bowls, in carrying case, c1930.
£20–30

A velvet cap embroidered 'BVGS', with tassel and braid, 1927–28
£30–40

Leather T-pattern football with lacing, c1940.
£40–50

Pigskin cartridge bag, with the initials 'H.G.P.' on the flap, c1930.
£45–55

A Don Bradman 'Club' cricket bat, c1930.
£55–60

'Wimbledon' fishtail lawn tennis racquet with original gut, c1910.
£80–120

Guide to Styles

Many objects are not marked or dated and their style is therefore an important clue to identification. Style is not always easy to pin down but the following pages may give you an idea of the 'look' that prevailed in the main periods from early Georgian through to the Sixties.

Often, a stylistic fashion will be a reaction against the previous trend, so that the cabriole legs of early Georgian furniture are succeeded by straight legs, and the curving naturalistic forms of Art Nouveau are replaced by the angular, geometric forms of Art Deco. However, a style that is rejected as unfashionable by the succeeding generation may then be revived by a later one.

Different materials, or combinations of perhaps the use of light woods instead of dark, or the use of inlay, may go hand in hand with changes in style. Changing technologies, and the introduction of new materials, influenced and formed new styles. It would be

hard to think of Art Deco without Bakelite and chrome, or the Sixties without plastic. The space race and scientific break-throughs are tangible influences on forms and style in the Sixties.

Politics and feelings of national identity also influenced style. When Pugin chose Gothic as the style for the Houses of Parliament he established it as the English national style. After WWII, the Festival of Britain introduced an instantly recognizable national style, epitomised by the famous Skylon, which often appears as a motif.

By the end of the 19th century many style influences came from abroad as the great trade exhibitions in London, Paris and New York internation-alized new ideas and ground-breaking techniques. Some of the most exciting design innovations in the applied arts came from the Wiener Werkstätte (a group of collaborating artists) in Vienna in the early 1900s.

The early years of the 20th century saw the beginning of the cult of the designer, with names like Tiffany still resonant. It also saw famous retailers such as Heals and Liberty selling fashionable brands like Lalique and Örrefors, to the masses.

Scandinavian designers, especially of furniture and glass, such as Alvar Aalto, played a major role in developing what we now think of as a 'modern' style.

KINGS & QUEENS

George I	1714–27
George II	1727–60
George III	1760–1811
Regency	1812–20
George IV	1820–30
William IV	1830–37
Victoria	1837–1901
Edward VII	1901–10
George V	1865–1936
George VI	1895–1952
Queen Elizabeth II	1926–

PERIODS AND DATES

Georgian
1714–1837
Classical styles and the golden age of furniture making.

Victorian
1837–1901
Decorative and opulent with many style revivals.

Art Nouveau
1880s–1920s
Sinuous, naturalistic forms often highly stylized.

Art Deco
1920s & '30s
Angular, geometric shapes and patterns.

Forties
Wartime austerity and the arrival of utility in design.

Fifties
The Festival of Britain and the birth of kitsch.

Sixties
Psychedelic patterns, high fashion and rise of the designer.

Early Georgian

The early 18th century saw cabriole legs and serpentine backs being replaced by a more ordered classical style based on the books of the Italian architect Palladio. It saw the transition from walnut to mahogany as the fashionable wood of choice. Classical motifs used for decoration underlined a connection with ancient Rome as a world power. It was also the 'Golden age' of English clockmaking. In the 1740s and 50s there was a stylistic revolt against classical order with two asymmetrical, extravagant styles: rococo and chinoiserie.

DESIGNERS

William Kent	1685–1748
Paul de Lamerie	1688–1751
George Wickes	1698–1761
Hubert Gravelot	1699–1773
William Linnell	1703–63
John Linnell	1729–96
George Graham	1773–1851
Matthias Lock (dates unknown)	

STYLE FEATURES

- Note the difference with later Georgian (*above*) Adam-style furniture with finer lines and classical detail.
- Serpentine backs and cabriole legs replaced by Palladian (classical) style.
- The 1740s rococo style is typified by asymmetrical C scrolls and naturalistic motifs.

Rococo figure with asymmetrical 'C' scroll base and naturalistic motifs.

Above: Similar shapes used for silver and ceramic teapots, latter decorated in Japanese style.

Mirror has similar serpentine top to the chair. Walnut veneer (also used for chests) popular in early 18th-century.

Ebonized (black stained) wood fashionable for clock cases.

Note the cabriole legs used on both the chest on stand and dining chair.

Late Georgian/ Regency

Under George III neo-classicism emerged as the predominant style, based on archaological discoveries at Herculaneum and Pompeii. It was finer and more restrained than Palladian classicism. The Gothic revival of the 1780s reflected a preference for home-grown styles. Both styles are reflected in the work of the great English furniture makers: Chippendale, Sheraton and Hepplewhite. The reign of George IV, is associated with the exotic styles based on Oriental and Indian design used at Brighton Pavilion. However, Regency classicism also flourished.

DESIGNERS	
Horace Walpole	1717–97
Thomas Chippendale	1718–79
Sir William Chambers	1723–96
George Hepplewhite	1727–86
Robert Adam	1728–92
Josiah Wedgwood	1730–95
Josiah Spode	1733–97
James Wyatt	1746–1813
Thomas Sheraton	1751–1806
Thomas Daniel	1749–1840
William Daniel	1769–1837
Thomas Hope	1769–1831
George Chinnery	1774–1852
Frederick Crace	1779–1859

The straight-sided silver shape is typical of the period.

Teapot using the same silver shape, decorated with clasically-inspired panels.

New bowfronted shape with ring handles, mahogany the wood of choice.

The brass inlay is a typical feature of regency furniture, as are the classically inspired curved sabre legs and gadrooned cresting.

Regency classicism is heavier and more grandiose.

Showy cut glass bonbonnières in classic covered vase shape.

Naturalistic motifs combined with classically inspired handle.

Supper set transfer-printed with scenes discovered in the excavations at Herculaneum. The shapes, too, are classically inspired.

Ebonized and gilded chair in Regency classical style based on Roman model.

Pembroke tables are a Georgian invention; this one has a pedestal base.

Gothic shape of case combined with Regency brass inlay using Gothic motifs.

Victorian

Typified by nostalgia and a love of decoration, styles became increasingly ornate during Queen Victoria's long reign. Characterized by a string of style revivals from Gothic, French Louis XV to medieval, they borrowed from sources as disparate as French rococo, the Italian Renaissance, Japan and Classical Greece. Increasing prosperity fuelled greater demand for furniture and all the decorative arts which, although there are many good quality pieces, was largely met by increased industrial mass-production, leading to a fall in quality.

Minton majolica – style borrowed from Italian Renaissance majolica.

DESIGNERS

Owen Jones	1809–74
A. W. N. Pugin	1812–52
William Burges	1827–81
E. W. Godwin	1833–86
Frederic, Lord Leighton	1830–96
Thomas Jeckyll	1827–81
Arthur Lasenby Liberty	1843–1917

STYLE FEATURES

• Love of decoration: ornate forms as well as surface decoration such as japanned (varnished) papier mâché, marquetry, parquetry and painted decoration with gilding.
• Colours are rich and opulent.
• Upholstery often ornate – buttoned, swagged, tasseled, fringed.
• The rise of the department store (eg Liberty's) and the birth of the mail order catalogue made styles available to all.

Attractive wood (here flame mahogany) and carved decoration typical.

Cranberry glass épergne in typically ornate, not to say fussy, style.

Victorian Gothic-revival style – always more robust than Georgian Gothic.

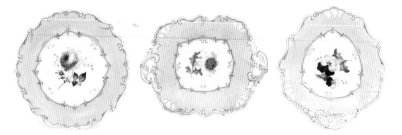

Dessert plates reflect interest in botany and show influence of Sèvres.

Typical floral-design papier mâché.

Arts & Crafts

Movement founded by William Morris and others as a reaction against increased industrialization and decorative excess. In 1861 Morris founded the company that became Morris & Co, making furniture, textiles, metalwork, ceramics, glass and wallpaper. Based on socialist principles, and a belief in the nobility of labour and creative freedom, they looked back to the Middle Ages as a period when forms were based on their use and decoration was simpler. Their ambition was to make widely available hand-crafted, quality products, made from honest materials. Their products, however, were expensive and they justified them through their philanthropic attitude to their employees. They also established craft guilds around the country, most famously the Art Workers Guild and the Guild of Handicraft. Their ideas were disseminated throughout the world in *The Studio* magazine.

DESIGNERS

William Morris	1834–96
Arthur Mackmurdo	1851–1942
C. F. A. Voysey	1857–1941
C. R. Ashbee	1863–1942
William Lethaby	1857–1931
William de Morgan	1839–1917
Jessie M. King	1873–1949

Oak dresser with foliate carving on the doors. Note the shape of the back.

C. R. Ashbee dish. The flowing handles are typical as is the enamel lid with pearl knop.

This armchair is mahogany but oak was often used. The elongation is typical.

STYLE FEATURES

Forms tend to be simple, dictated by use, often with stylized decoration. Motifs are often natural (flora or fauna) but were also borrowed from medieval and Islamic art. Objects are often not highly finished, eg hammering visible in metalwork.

- William de Morgan tiles (*above*) influenced by Islamic art. One of the most innovative ceramic designers.
- Influence of retailers such as Liberty & Co and Heals & Sons in distributing objects in the Arts & Crafts style.

Silver-plated copper casket. Note the finish – hammering is visible on the lid.

Brannam Pottery many-handled drinking vessel makes use of a medieval form.

Art Nouveau

Art Nouveau can be seen as the first 'modern' international style emerging fully fledged at the Paris Universal Exhibition of 1900. It was soon the fashionable style all over Europe and America, not just in the decorative arts but also in architecture and interior decoration. Its inspiration is in nature, but stylized and transformed into sometimes bizarre shapes. It exploited technological advances not only in materials and manufacturing but also in, for example, electric lighting for Tiffany's stained glass lamps. Art Nouveau is all about consumer consumption of luxury goods and was enthusiastically propagated by department stores like Liberty's – it was known in Italy as 'Stile Liberty'. It is linked with *fin de siècle* decadence and came to an end with the First World War.

Gilt-bronze figure of a woman. The clinging draperies, flowing hair and posture are typical. 'Dream maidens' were a popular motif.

Extreme stylization of natural forms and drapery-like folds to create a decorative effect. The elbow-like handles are very typical of Jugendstil (German Art Nouveau).

Female face and tendrils typical. Much more ornate than the casket on p143.

Loetz irridescent glass bowl. Note the sinuous brass stand.

Tiffany lamp. The patinated bronze used for the base was a popular material.

Oak smoker's cabinet. Note the twined forms of the brass inlay reminiscent of Celtic decoration and the effect of drapery down the sides.

Note the influence of Arts & Crafts chair design (*p143*), but more curvacious and decorative.

Pewter candlesticks. Pewter was a popular material with Art Nouveau designers. Note the shape of the handles.

The clock's splayed feet, domed top and pronounced cornice are typical. Decorated with stylized floral inlay.

Graphics became exaggerated and stylized especially for posters.

STYLE FEATURES

- Relatively inexpensive piece of silver and enamel jewellery by Charles Horner, similar to those sold by Liberty's.
- Sinuous, naturalistic forms often writhing and intertwined. Decoration is an end in itself. Another common motif is a female face or draped figure with tendril-like hair, often apparently in a trance-like state.
- Use of iridescent glass. Also many other innovatory glass techniques such as cameo glass or *pâte-de-verre* used to new decorative effect.
- New bulbous or attenuated shapes in glass and ceramics designed to accentuate the decoration.

Daum glass vase. Similar glass was also made by Gallé, and is very typical.

Art Deco

Created by Paris designers in the 1920s, Art Deco started as a luxury interior decoration style. It was a complete break with the past, a design aesthetic for the modern world, and was much influenced by contemporary art movements. Art Deco reflected the ideas of the 'modern movement' and the machine age and expressed them in geometric forms suited to industrial production. The style is instantly recognizable. Art Deco made use of expensive materials, as well as new materials such as ply, plastic, metal, chrome and Bakelite, which lent themselves to such a sculptural, hard-edged style. Moulded Bakelite was used for mass-produced items like radios, cameras and inexpensive jewellery, while moulded glass by makers such as Lalique, Baccarat and Daum was sold to a hungry public by fashion-conscious department stores.

Note the brightly coloured decoration and triangular form with angular handle.

<table>
<tr><td colspan="2">DESIGNERS</td></tr>
</table>

Jacques Emile Ruhlmann	1879–1933
Le Corbusier	1887–1965
Frank Lloyd Wright	1867–1959
William Van Alen	1883–1954
René Lalique	1860–1945
Clarice Cliff	1899–1972
Keith Murray	1892–1981
Susie Cooper	1902–95
Wells Coates	1895–1958
E. McKnight Kauffer	1890–1954
Eileen Gray	1879–1976
Sonia Delaunay	1885–1979
Alvar Aalto	1898–1976

Design influences included Egyptian and Cubist art, as well as the ideas of De Stijl, the Bauhaus and the Wiener Werkstätte.

Moulded *pâte-de-cristal* glass vase. Note the intersecting geometric shapes.

Deco shapes applied to a conventional silver teaset, with decorative rosewood handles.

Ingenious use of geometric forms. Walnut was a popular decorative wood.

The angularity of the face and figure are derived from Cubist art.

Streamlined figure with stylized swept-back hair and draperies typical of Art Deco. Unlike Art Nouveau women, these are amazons.

- Geometric forms are the hallmark of Art Deco, everything is angular.
- Shapes are bold and simple.
- Colours are often strong and contrasting, such as black and red, with chrome used to highlight features. Use of new materials like plastic and Bakelite.
- Speed was one of the technological advances of the age and is reflected in aerodynamic, streamlined designs such as the female figures with swept back hair set in a geometric pattern.

Double clip, very typical brooch shape of the period. Diamonds set in platinum rather than gold to give a cooler, harder look.

Mirrored-glass radio and contrasting chrome trim.

Stone lent itself to Art Deco's sharp lines. Note the rectangular face.

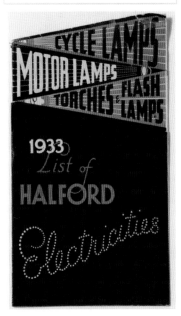

Strong contrasting colours are Art Deco, although shape is not.

Elaborate wrought-ironwork was a feature of many Art Deco interiors.

Eyecatching graphic design with triangular panels highlighting contents.

The Forties

With the advent of war in 1939 came an end to frivolity. Materials became scarce and many items, such as clothes and furniture, were rationed. Under government supervision designers, several of them grounded in the Arts & Crafts Movement's ideas of honesty and fitness for purpose, were asked to create simple, functional designs under the 'Utility' label. They also drew inspiration from Scandinavian designers of the 1930s. The Modernists continued to flourish in America using avant-garde materials like formica, tubular steel, aluminium and plywood, creating a stark 'Modern' look of which Utility is the poor relation.

Un-idealized 'ordinary' figures, often gently humorous, are typical.

DESIGNERS	
Walter Gropius	1883–1969
Mies van de Rohe	1886–1969
Alvar Aalto	1898–1976
Marcel Breuer	1902–81
Vicke Lindstrand	1904–83
Charles Eames	1907–78
Ray Eames	1912–88

Pared down design. Use of glass for the face, unframed by a case.

The Spitfire is one of the most iconic designs. Shades of Deco in the stand.

One of the first modern-style cameras.

Scandinavian designers, such as Örrefors, abandoned historical precedent and produced influential new pared-down glass shapes without decoration.

New ranges of kitchenware with minimal decoration and stark graphics.

Utility suit. The amount of fabric and buttons was strictly controlled.

Note the simple yet functional form of this metal desk lamp in gunmetal grey.

The Buick car is an iconic Forties shape.

Minimal production values, see tie, and very basic, functional graphics.

A watch shape that became a design classic, here with Art Deco undertones.

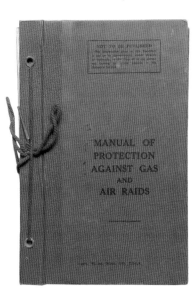

Oak-veneered plywood chairs. Simple pared-down design similar to Scandinavian designs. This period saw production of stacking chairs.

Growth of photography, here used to promote the glamour of US films.

The Fifties

After a decade of austerity, the Festival of Britain in 1951 was a 'tonic for the nation' and a chance to re-establish its national identity. It set out to give a feeling of recovery while at the same time promoting good design in the rebuilding of Britain. The Festival emphasized the importance of the arts and design. The cigar-shaped Skylon which dominated the Festival became a recurring motif in Fifties design, much of which is jokey. The Festival logo is a light-hearted combination of the four points of the compass with Britannia's profile and bunting in red, white and blue. The Fifies are also known for kitsch, cheap and gimicky often plastic objects which met consumer demand for amusing design. They also saw the rise of craft in the work of potters like Bernard Leach and Lucie Rie.

Abstract Festival pattern.

DESIGNERS	
Lucienne Day	1917–
Robin Day	1915–
Abram Games	1914–96
Hidalgo Moya	1920–94
Phillip Powell	1921–2003
Tapio Wirkkala	1915–85
Lucie Rie	1902–95
Bernard Leach	1887–1979

Tubular steel and foam rubber chair with characteristic upholstery design.

Cut glass reinvented with a striking modern geometric design.

Clean lines of Scandinavian-inspired design.

New 'Modernist' shapes with abstract geometric decoration.

Radio with simulated crocodile-skin case, echoing tastes in fashion. Crocodile handbags were popular because crocodile was not rationed.

- The distinctive shapes of Danish-designed cutlery were very influential.
- Many patterns are 'bitty' with small elements apparently randomly compiled.
- Use of abstract designs. Colours are often bright and bold.
- Range of new shapes, many of them inspired by Italian, American and Scandinavian design. Furniture shapes are often simple and pared down.

An illustrated review of British design at the Festival bearing the Festival logo.

Tin decorated with fun 'bitty' pattern and characteristic lighthearted graphics.

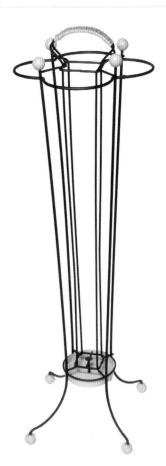

Potters like Lucie Rie and Bernard Leach used simple forms.

Characteristic Fifties colours used for a bold semi-abstract Scandinavian fabric design.

Kitsch wirework umbrella stand, typical of Fifties jokey design.

The Sixties

The Sixties saw the birth of youth culture and a more carefree approach to design. A new 'buy it today, throw it away tomorrow' culture emerged bolstered by a new economic prosperity. Goods aimed at the youth market had to be cheap and quality was therefore often low. Gimmicky designs caught the mood of the moment. Design was influenced by Op Art and Pop Art, by the space race, mind bending drugs and new scientific discoveries. Television sets were designed that looked like space helmets, psychedelic patterns for wallpapers and fabrics and innovatory graphic designs. Mary Quant's mini skirt and the department store Biba set new standards of fashion design. For many designers of the period, plastics from PVC to Perspex were the materials of choice which could be moulded and injected to create a variety of bright colours and bold forms.

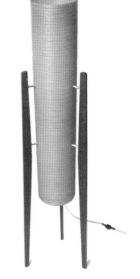

Spun fibre and teak 'rocket' floor lamp inspired by the space race.

DESIGNERS	
Mary Quant	1934–
Barbara Hulaniki (Biba)	1936–
Malcolm Sayer (E-type)	1916–70
Derek Birdsall	1934–
Alec Issigonis (Mini)	1906–88
Terence Conran	1931–
Kenneth Grange	1929–
Max Clendinning	1934-
Wolff Olins	1965-
Robin Day	1915–
David Mellor	1930–
Alex Moulton	1920–

Eye catching geometric designs typical of period. Here a Danish carpet design.

New more dramatic approach to graphics characteristic of the period.

Less serious than the ply chairs of the 1950s, (*see p149*) these laminated walnut chairs are upholstered in bright blue vinyl, much used for upholstery in the Sixties.

You can see it has 1950s antecedents, but its metal supports are very 1960s.

• Orange is a very Sixties colour, here combined with the textured surface and ideosyncratic shape typical of Whitefriars.
• Use of bright colours, such as orange or bright blue, and extravagant shapes. Psychedelic patterns used for fabrics, paper and wallpaper. Interest in texture for both glass and pottery.
• 1960s jewellery often big and over-the-top – large rings, long dangly earrings – much of it plastic. Fashion one of the key design areas of the period.
• Wacky, quality objects were meant to be ephemeral.

Tall dramatic shape and the wave-like surface creating patterns in the thick glass are typical.

A lot of use was made of and patterned textured surfaces.

Wacky films reflected the carefree attitude to life and was reflected in design.

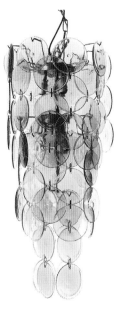

Synthetic fabrics were very fashionable, here with a psychedelic pattern.

Mod sunglasses with characteristic Sixties styling and funky Op Art frames.

Light employing a favourite 1960s chain mail or overlapping disc motifs.

Glossary

acanthus: Leaf motif, used in carved decoration and metal mounts.

anchor escapement: Said to have been invented c1670 by Robert Hooke or William Clement. A type of escape mechanism shaped like an anchor, which engages at precise intervals with the toothed escape wheel. The anchor permits the use of a pendulum (either long or short), and gives greater accuracy than was possible with the verge escapement.

bezel: Ring, usually brass, surrounding the dial of a clock, and securing the glass dial cover.

bisque: French term for biscuit ware, or unglazed porcelain.

body: The material from which pottery or porcelain is made (although the term paste is more often used for porcelain). Also refers to the main part of a piece.

bracket clock: A type of spring-driven clock designed to stand on a bracket or table.

Britannia standard: Higher standard of silver required between 1697 and 1720. Denoted by Britannia and a lion's head in profile on the hallmark.

cabriole leg: Outwardly curving S-shaped leg, popular from late 17thC onwards.

cameo glass: Two or more layers of coloured glass in which the top layer/s are then cut or etched away to create a multi-coloured design in relief. An ancient technique popular with Art Nouveau glassmakers in the early 20thC.

carriage clock: A small spring-driven portable clock, usually with a brass frame and glazed sides and back, produced mainly by French makers during the 19thC.

cased glass: One layer of glass, often coloured, sandwiched between two plain glass layers or vice versa, the outer layer engraved to create a decorative effect. An ancient technique revived in the 19thC. See **cameo glass.**

chinoiserie: The fashion, prevailing in the late 18thC, for Chinese-style ornamentation on porcelain, wallpapers, fabrics, furniture and garden architecture.

clock garniture: Matching group of clock and vases or candelabra for the mantel shelf. Often highly ornate.

cloisonné: Enamelling on metal with divisions in the design separated by lines of fine metal wire. A speciality of the Limoges region of France in the Middle Ages, and of Chinese craftsmen to the present day.

crizzling: Where an imbalance in the glass batch has caused the surface of the glass to become fogged by a network of tiny cracks.

deadbeat escapement: Type of anchor escapement, possibly invented by George Graham and used in precision pendulum clocks.

ebonized: Wood stained and polished black to simulate ebony.

enamel: A glossy, opaque, hard protective coating. Invariably hand-painted, colours are permanent and cannot fade, with the exception being turquoise blue.

escapement: That part of the clock that regulates it transmits the impulse of the wheel train to the pendulum or balance.

flatware: Cutlery.

fluted: Border that resembles a scalloped edge, used as a decoration on furniture, glass, silver and porcelain.

fusee: 18thC clockwork invention; a cone-shaped drum, linked to the spring barrel by a length of gut or chain. The shape compensates for the declining strength of the mainspring thus ensuring constant timekeeping.

hard paste: True porcelain made of china stone (petuntse) and kaolin; the formula was long known to, and kept secret by, Chinese potters but only discovered in the 1720s at Meissen, Germany, from where it spread to the rest of Europe and the Americas. Recognized by its hard, glossy feel.

gesso: A plaster-like substance applied to carved furniture before gilding, also used as a substitute for carving when moulded and applied.

gouache: Opaque watercolour paint in which the pigments are bound with glue and the lighter tones contain white.

Imari: Export Japanese porcelain of predominantly red, blue and gold decoration which, although made in Arita, is named after the port from which it was shipped.

ironstone: Stoneware, patented in 1813 by Charles James Mason, containing ground glassy slag, a by-product of iron smelting, for extra strength.

latticinio: Fine threads of white or clear glass forming a filigree mesh effect enclosed in clear glass.

lead crystal: Glass made using a large proportion of lead oxide that was not vulnerable to **crizzling**, first made by George Ravenscroft in the late 17thC.

longcase clock: A floor standing clock, with anchor escapement, of 30-hour or 8-day duration. Also known as a grandfather clock, a grandmother clock being a smaller version.

mantel clock: A small bracket or table clock, typically in a rosewood, mahogany, ebonized or gilded case, produced mainly in the 19thC.

marquetry: Decorative inlay, usually with floral motifs, using veneers of variously coloured woods.

marriage: Joining together of two unrelated parts to form one piece of furniture.

mother-of-pearl: A hard iridescent substance, forms the inner layer of certain mollusc shells, such as oyster. Used to inlay furniture, make buttons etc.

mystery clock: A clock whose way of working is deliberately obscure.

ormolu: Strictly, gilded bronze but used loosely for any yellow metal. Originally used for furniture handles and mounts but, from the 18thC, for inkstands, candlesticks etc.

parquetry: Form of inlay using different coloured woods to form a geometric pattern.

pearlware: A fine earthenware, similar to creamware but with a decided blue tint to the glaze. Although developed by Wedgwood in about 1779, it was soon adopted by all the major potters in England and Wales.

plique-à-jour: Enamelling technique in which a structure of metal strips is laid on a metal background to form enclosed areas which are then filled with transparent enamels. When the backing is removed, a transparent 'stained glass' effect is achieved.

repoussé: Relief decoration on metal made by hammering on the reverse so that the decoration projects.

roemer: German spelling of 19thC English low drinking goblet.

sabre leg: Curved chair leg resembling the line of a sabre blade, popular duing the Regency period.

soft paste: Artificial porcelain made with the addition of ground glass, bone-ash or soap-stone. Used by most European porcelain manufacturers during the 18thC. Recognized by its soft, soapy feel.

spelter: Zinc treated to look like bronze and much used as an inexpensive substitute in Art Nouveau appliqué ornament and Art Deco figures.

timepiece: Clock that does not strike or chime.

touch: Maker's mark stamped on much, but not all, early English pewter, and was strictly controlled by the Pewterer's Company of London: early examples consist of initials, later ones are more elaborate and pictorial.

veneer: Thin layer of decorative wood glued to the carcase of a piece of furniture.

verge escapement: Oldest form of escapement, found on clocks as early as 1300 and still in use in 1900. Consisting of a bar (the verge) with two flag-shaped pallets that rock in and out of the teeth of the crown or escape wheel to regulate the movement.

vitrine: French display cabinet often of bombé or serpentine outline and ornately decorated.

Bibliography

Bannister, Judith, **English Silver Hallmarks**, *Foulsham, 1999*

Battersby, Martin, **The Decorative Twenties**, *Herbert Press, 1988*

Battersby, Martin, **The Decorative Thirties**, *Herbert Press, 1988*

Bly, John, **Discovering Hallmarks on English Silver**, *Shire, 2000*

A. W. Coysh and R. Henrywood, **The Dictionary of Blue and White Printed Pottery 1780–1880**, *2 volumes, Antique Collectors' Club*

Fiell, Charlotte & Peter, **Design Handbook**, *Taschen, 2006*

Godden, Geoffrey A., **Godden's Guide to English Blue & White Porcelain**, *Antique Collectors' Club, 1999*

Godden, Geoffrey A., **Godden's Guide to Ironstone, Stone & Granite Wares**, *Antique Collectors' Club, 1999*

Godden, Geoffrey A., **New Guide to English Porcelain**, *London, Octopus Publishing Group, 2004*

Godden, Geoffrey A., **New Handbook of British Pottery & Porcelain Marks**, *Ebury Press, 1999*

Higgins, Katherine, **Are you Rich?**, *Andre Deutsch, 1999*

Jackson, Anna, **Period Styles**, *V&A Publications, 2002*

Klein, Dan, McClelland, N. & Haslam, M., **The Deco Style**, *Thames & Hudson, 1987*

Knowles, Eric, **Victoriana to Art Deco**, *Millers, 1993*

Mallalieu, H.L., **Dictionary of Watercolour Artists**, *Antiques Collectors Club, 1999*

McConnell, Andy, **20th-Century Glass**, *Millers, 2006*

McConnell, Andy, **The Decanter: An Illustrated History of Glass from 1650**, *Antique Collectors' Club, 2004*

Miller's Antiques Encyclopedia

Miller's Antiques Price Guide 2008

Miller's Antiques Price Guide 2007

Miller's Art Nouveau & Art Deco Buyer's Guide

Miller's Ceramics Buyer's Guide

Miller's Clocks & Barometers Buyer's Guide

Miller's Collectables Price Guide 2007

Miller's Collectables Price Guide 2008

Miller's Collecting Pottery & Porcelain The Facts at Your Fingertips

Miller's Dolls and Teddy Bears Antiques Checklist

Miller's Glass Antiques Checklist

Miller's Glass Buyer's Guide

Miller's Pictures Price Guide New Edition

Miller's Pictures Price Guide 2004

Miller's Silver & Plate Buyer's Guide

Miller's Silver & Sheffield Plate Marks

Miners, Steven, **Costume Jewellery**, *Millers, 2006*

Neale, Gillian, **Collecting Blue & White Pottery**, *Millers, 2004*

Neale, Gillian, **Encyclopeadia of British Transfer-printed Pottery Patterns 1790–1930**, *Millers, 2005*

Payne, Christopher, **Miller's Collecting Furniture**, *London, Mitchell Beazley, 1998*

Pearson, Sue, **Miller's Teddy Bears, A Complete Collector's Guide**, *London, Octopus Publishing Group, 2001*

Sandon, John, **Miller's Collecting Porcelain**, *London, Octopus Publishing Group, 2003*

Snodin, Michael & Styles, J., **Georgian Britain 1714–1837**, *V&A Publications, 2004*

Snodin, Michael & Styles, J., **Victorian Britain 1837–1901**, *V&A Publications, 2004*

Snodin, Michael & Styles, J., **Design and the Decorative Arts in Britain 1500–1900**, *V&A Publications, 2001*

Tozzo, Pepe, **Collectable Technology**, *Carlton Books, 2005*

Index